T0332635

INCREMENTAL VERSION-SPACE MERGING: A General Framework for Concept Learning

THE KLUWER INTERNATIONAL SERIES
IN ENGINEERING AND COMPUTER SCIENCE

KNOWLEDGE REPRESENTATION, LEARNING AND EXPERT SYSTEMS

Consulting Editor

Tom Mitchell
Carnegie Mellon University

Other books in the series:

UNIVERSAL SUBGOALING AND CHUNKING OF GOAL HIERARCHIES, J. Laird,
P. Rosenbloom, A. Newell
  ISBN: 0-89838-213-0

MACHINE LEARNING: A Guide to Current Research, T. Mitchell, J. Carbonell,
R. Michalski
  ISBN: 0-89838-214-9

MACHINE LEARNING OF INDUCTIVE BIAS, P. Utgoff
  ISBN: 0-89838-223-8

A CONNECTIONIST MACHINE FOR GENETIC HILLCLIMBING, D. H. Ackley
  ISBN: 0-89838-236-X

LEARNING FROM GOOD AND BAD DATA, P. D. Laird
  ISBN: 0-89838-263-7

MACHINE LEARNING OF ROBOT ASSEMBLY PLANS, A. M. Segre
  ISBN: 0-89838-269-6

AUTOMATING KNOWLEDGE ACQUISITION FOR EXPERT SYSTEMS,
S. Marcus, Editor
  ISBN: 0-89838-294-7

MACHINE LEARNING, META-REASONING AND LOGICS, P. B. Brazdil,
K. Konolige
  ISBN: 0-7923-9047-4

CHANGE OF REPRESENTATION AND INDUCTIVE BIAS: D. P. Benjamin
  ISBN: 0-7923-9055-5

KNOWLEDGE ACQUISITION: SELECTED RESEARCH AND COMMENTARY,
S. Marcus, Editor
  ISBN: 0-7923-9062-8

LEARNING WITH NESTED GENERALIZED EXEMPLARS, S. L. Salzberg
  ISBN: 0-7923-9110-1

INCREMENTAL VERSION-SPACE MERGING: A General Framework for Concept Learning

by

Haym Hirsh
Rutgers University

KLUWER ACADEMIC PUBLISHERS
Boston/Dordrecht/London

Distributors for North America:
Kluwer Academic Publishers
101 Philip Drive
Assinippi Park
Norwell, Massachusetts 02061 USA

Distributors for all other countries:
Kluwer Academic Publishers Group
Distribution Centre
Post Office Box 322
3300 AH Dordrecht, THE NETHERLANDS

Library of Congress Cataloging-in-Publication Data

Hirsh, Haym, 1963–
    Incremental version-space merging : a general framework for
concept learning / by Haym Hirsh.
        p. cm. — (The Kluwer international series in engineering and
computer science. Knowledge representation, learning, and expert
systems)
    Includes bibliographical references and index.
    ISBN 0–7923–9119–5
    1. Machine learning.   2. Artificial intelligence.   3. Cognitive
science.   I. Title.   II. Series.
Q325.5.H57   1990
006.3—dc20   90–37918
                                                        CIP

Printed in the United States of America

Contents

Foreword

One of the most enjoyable experiences in science is hearing a simple but novel idea which instantly rings true, and whose consequences then begin to unfold in unforeseen directions. For me, this book presents such an idea and several of its ramifications.

This book is concerned with machine learning. It focuses on a question that is central to understanding how computers might learn: "how can a computer acquire the definition of some general concept by abstracting from specific training instances of the concept?" Although this question of how to automatically generalize from examples has been considered by many researchers over several decades, it remains only partly answered. The approach developed in this book, based on Haym Hirsh's Ph.D. dissertation, leads to an algorithm which efficiently and exhaustively searches a space of hypotheses (possible generalizations of the data) to find all maximally consistent hypotheses, even in the presence of certain types of inconsistencies in the data. More generally, it provides a framework for integrating different types of constraints (e.g., training examples, prior knowledge) which allow the learner to reduce the set of hypotheses under consideration.

Hirsh's approach to this learning task is an extension to the *version space* approach, originally proposed ten years earlier in my own Ph.D. dissertation. A version space may be defined simply as follows: given a language of candidate hypotheses and a set of training examples, the version space is the set of all hypotheses from the language that are consistent with these training examples. It turns out that the version space can be efficiently represented by its maximally specific members and its maximally general members. Furthermore, a learning procedure exists which efficiently updates this representation of the version space to remove candidate hypotheses found inconsistent with newly encountered training examples. As data accumulate, the version space of acceptable hypotheses shrinks until only a single hypothesis remains: the learned concept.

This learning algorithm based on version spaces has the attractive property that it is guaranteed to converge to a correctly learned concept given an appropriate hypothesis language and sufficient training data. However, it has not gained widespread use in practice, largely due to the fact that it cannot accommodate inconsistent or noisy training data, and it cannot make use of prior knowledge of the learner to guide its generalization algorithm. Because of these shortcomings, it has been supplanted by other methods which overcome these limitations but lack its completeness and convergence properties.

Hirsh's work takes a significant step toward removing both of these limitations. His extension to the approach allows accommodating certain types of inconsistent training data, while preserving the convergence properties of the learning method. He also shows how prior knowledge can be used to preprocess and generalize training examples (via a method called explanation-based generalization), to form more powerful constraints which are then used to reduce the version space of remaining hypotheses.

The basis for these extensions is Hirsh's insight that the version space approach could be generalized by changing the fundamental operation from that of shrinking the version space in response to a new training example, to the operation of intersecting two version spaces. This change requires that each new constraint for reducing the current version space be itself first represented as a version space. But by changing to this uniform representation of constraints, the generalized approach gains the ability to accommodate a broader range of constraints and methods for preprocessing the training data.

This idea of representing all incoming constraints themselves in terms of version spaces is the simple, obvious (in retrospect!) idea which lies at the heart of this book. And the consequences of this idea, elaborated in the following chapters, lead to a surprising approach to handling certain types of noisy training data, to a method for combining results of learning from multiple subsets of training data, and to a means of combining inductive and explanation-based learning methods. Hirsh's approach is rigorously defined, and its ramifications are explored both experimentally and analytically. Experimental results show the practical significance of the approach, including the performance of the learning algorithm on noisy data. Theoretical analysis reveals both the conceptual foundations of the approach and the computational complexity of the associated algorithms.

If the foreword of the book is to provide a bit of background and a bit of motivation for the potential reader, then perhaps I am in a good position to write this one. In the ten years since version spaces were introduced, I have read a fair number of papers proposing extensions and providing analyses. Of all these, the one that has most taken me by surprise is the book you hold in your hands. For all my looking, I simply had not foreseen that this generalization of the approach would lead so directly to the extensions presented here. I am pleased to find it so. And it kindles my curiosity as to what other surprises might follow!

Tom M. Mitchell
Pittsburgh, PA

Preface

The problem of concept learning—forming general rules from examples—has received much attention in artificial intelligence. Among the most influential approaches to this problem is Mitchell's work on version spaces, which implemented learning as a search process through the space of hypotheses that would correctly classify the training data. However, its inability to consider candidate generalizations that are not strictly consistent with the data has limited the practical utility of version spaces.

This book presents a generalization of Mitchell's version-space approach to concept learning that partially removes this limitation. It presents the generalized approach and its application to a number of learning tasks, including problems of learning from noisy data and integrating background knowledge into the learning process.

This book is an updated version of my doctoral dissertation, and I am indebted to a great number of people who made its completion possible. I am most grateful to my Stanford reading committee. As an advisor Bruce Buchanan helped me overcome my unfamiliarity with the terrain and succeed; as head of the Helix Group of the KSL he provided an excellent work environment. Tom Mitchell's contribution to this thesis could have stopped with his past work, upon which this dissertation is almost totally based. I am glad it did not; discussions with him about version spaces and explanation-based learning had a great impact on this work, as did his arrangement of facilities at Carnegie Mellon University for the final year of this work. Finally, I have greatly valued discussions with and feedback from Paul Rosenbloom on this and other work over the years; his insightful comments have been a principal reason for the success of this work.

Others who have had an impact on this work include David Aha, Jim

Blythe, Tze-Pin Cheng, Scott Clearwater, William Cohen, Tom Dietterich, Oren Etzioni, Nick Flann, Benjamin Grosof, David Haussler, Rich Keller, Stuart Russell, Jeff Schlimmer, Johanna Seibt, Derek Sleeman, Dave Smith, Devika Subramanian, John Sullivan, Paul Utgoff, Monte Zweben, members of the GRAIL and Logic groups at Stanford and the MLRG group at CMU, and the many friends I've made over the years at Stanford, Pittsburgh, and Rutgers. The technical, financial, and administrative support of the Stanford Computer Science Department, Stanford Knowledge Systems Laboratory, CMU School of Computer Science, University of Pittsburgh Intelligent Systems Laboratory, and Rutgers Computer Science Department is greatly appreciated.

Final thanks, however, must go to my family, who ultimately made this work possible.

INCREMENTAL VERSION-SPACE MERGING: A General Framework for Concept Learning

Chapter 1

Overview

The power of an intelligent system lies in its knowledge. Much of the work in artificial intelligence has been on the acquisition of such knowledge for intelligent systems (e.g., Davis and Lenat, 1982; Marcus, 1988). This work addresses the task of inferring knowledge by generalization—forming general rules from specific cases. Cases are viewed as examples of some unknown concept, and the problem is thus to find a definition of the concept given known positive and negative examples of the concept. This *concept learning* approach to knowledge acquisition has received much attention in the machine learning community over the years (Buchanan and Mitchell, 1978; Michalski and Chilausky, 1980; Mitchell *et al.*, 1983; Quinlan, 1983).

   Concept learning can be viewed as a problem of search (Simon and Lea, 1974; Mitchell, 1978, 1982)—to identify some concept definition out of a space of possible definitions. Mitchell (1978) formalizes this view of *generalization as search* in his development of *version spaces*. He defines a version space to be the set of all concept definitions in a prespecified language that correctly classify training data—the positive and negative examples of the unknown concept. Although a landmark work, it was limited in its underlying assumption that the desired concept definition will be consistent with all the given data.

   This book presents a generalization of Mitchell's version-space approach to concept learning that takes it beyond strict consistency with data. The generality of this new version-space framework is demonstrated by its

1

use in four very different learning tasks. Two of these stand as contributions in their own right, solving open problems for machine learning. The first is a computationally feasible approach to learning from inconsistent data with version spaces. The second is a combination of two classical approaches to concept learning—empirical and analytical learning—that solves some of the problems that they each have when used in isolation. Most notable is the fact that all four learning tasks solved within the generalized version-space framework use a single concept-learning method, *incremental version-space merging*, developed as part of the framework and implemented in the program IVSM (included in the appendix).

This chapter begins with a brief review of the version-space approach to concept learning. An overview of the three principal contributions of this work is then presented. The chapter concludes with a guide to the rest of the book.

1.1   Background: Version Spaces and the Candidate-Elimination Algorithm

Given a set of training data and a language in which the desired concept must be expressed (which defines the space of possible generalizations concept learning will search), Mitchell (1977, 1978) defines a version space to be "the set of all concept descriptions within the given language which are consistent with those training instances" (Mitchell, 1978). Mitchell noted that the generality of concepts imposes a partial order that allows efficient representation of the version space by the boundary sets S and G representing the most specific and most general concept definitions in the space. The S- and G-sets delimit the set of all concept definitions consistent with the given data—the version space contains all concepts as or more general than some element in S and as or more specific than some element in G.

Given a new instance, some of the concept definitions in the version space for past data may not classify it correctly. The *candidate-elimination algorithm* manipulates the boundary-set representation of a version space to create boundary sets that represent a new version space consistent with all the previous instances plus the new one. For a positive example of the unknown concept the algorithm generalizes the elements of the S-set as little as possible so that they cover the new instance yet remain consistent with past data, and removes those elements of the G-set that do not cover the new instance. For a negative instance the algorithm specializes elements of the G-set so that they no longer cover the new instance yet remain consistent with past data, and removes from the S-set those elements that mistakenly cover the new, negative instance. The unknown concept is determined when the version space has only one element, which in the boundary-set representation is when the S- and G-sets have the same single element.

The assumption of strict consistency with data is a major limitation for the version-space approach to concept learning. When no concept definition in the description language can distinguish between all the positive examples and all the negative examples, the data are said to be *inconsistent* with respect to the concept description language. In such cases the version space collapses—the algorithm halts, unable to generate any plausible concept definitions. The problem is that some instance causes the desired definition to be removed from consideration.

Furthermore, strict consistency with data—by definition—limits the ability to incorporate in a general way outside knowledge of a domain into learning. Given the commonsense knowledge that a domain expert brings to bear—the knowledge that allows an expert to immediately recognize that a rule is nonsensical in the given domain—strict consistency with data precludes incorporating the knowledge into learning. This work generalizes the version-space approach to concept learning so that it can partially overcome these shortcomings.

1.2 Contributions

This section briefly reviews the main contributions of this work, which will be developed in detail in subsequent chapters. They are the generalized version-space framework, and the solution to two learning tasks within this framework: learning from inconsistent data, and combining empirical and analytical learning.

1.2.1   Incremental Version-Space Merging

There were two principal insights in Mitchell's work. The first was to consider and keep track of a set of candidate concept definitions, rather than keeping a single definition deemed best thus far. The second insight was that the set of all concept definitions need not be explicitly enumerated and maintained, but rather the partial ordering on concepts could be exploited to provide an efficient means of representation for the space of concept definitions. The key idea in this work is to maintain Mitchell's two insights, but remove its assumption of strict consistency with training data—a version space is generalized to be any set of concept definitions in a concept description language representable by boundary sets.

The principal contribution of this portion of the book is a general framework for concept learning that generalizes Mitchell's notion of version space beyond strict consistency with data. The generalized framework has firm theoretical underpinnings, and central to it is an incremental learning method based on version-space intersection. Given a version space based on one set of information, and another based on a second set of information, the intersection of the two version spaces reflects the union of the sets of information. Such version-space intersection forms the basis for the incremental learning method, called *incremental version-space merging*, developed as part of this work. When new information is obtained, incremental version-space merging forms the version space of concept definitions that are relevant given the new information and intersects it with the version space for past information. The key observation is that concept learning can be viewed as the two-step process of specifying sets of relevant concept definitions and intersecting these sets.

The insight from which the generality of incremental version-space merging arises is that the specific learning task should define how each piece of information is to be interpreted—what the version space of relevant concept definitions should be. Each piece of information (such as a training instance and its classification) imposes some constraint on which concept definitions may be considered, and thus can be viewed as specifying some set of legal concept definitions. Intersecting the resulting sets across all pieces of information yields those concept definitions that no piece of information rules out.

1.2.2 Learning from Inconsistent Data

The second contribution of this work is an approach to the problem of concept learning given inconsistent data using version spaces. Mitchell (1978) suggested one solution to this problem that is of theoretical interest. He proposes forming generalizations consistent with subsets of the original training data. The difficulty with the approach is that it is unknown which subset is the desired one, so the learning system must keep track of concept definitions consistent with many different subsets of the data. This is computationally costly, and thus the problem here is to learn from inconsistent data in a manner that is computationally feasible.

The approach taken here is to forego a solution to the full problem of learning from inconsistent data, and instead solve a subcase of the problem for one particular class of inconsistency that can be exploited in learning. The underlying assumption for this class of inconsistency, called bounded inconsistency, is that some small perturbation to the description of any bad instance will result in a good instance (such as when misclassifications are due to small measurement errors). When this is true, a learning system can search through the space of concept definitions that correctly classify either the original data, or small perturbations of the data. The version space will contain all concept definitions consistent with either each instance or some neighbor of each instance. The difficulty version spaces have with inconsistent data is that some instance causes the desired definition to be removed from consideration. Here a larger number of concept definitions are kept in consideration to decrease the chance of this happening. Although this cannot handle random classification errors—when even perfect training data are occasionally labeled incorrectly—it does handle the case in which a bad example is never very far from a good one.

1.2.3 Combining Empirical and Analytical Learning

Incremental version-space merging is an example of *empirical learning* (also known as *similarity-based learning*). Such systems find concept descriptions that best classify a set of training data without the use of an extensive theory of the domain. In contrast, the more recent work on *analytical learning* (also known as *explanation-based learning*) (Mitchell *et al.*,

1986; DeJong and Mooney, 1986) relies on strong knowledge of a domain. This knowledge is typically used to analyze a single instance, and the result is used as the basis for a generalization of the instance consistent with the knowledge. The final contribution of this work is using the version-space framework to combine empirical and analytical learning. The central idea is to first apply analytical learning to training data, and then apply empirical learning (as done by incremental version-space merging) to the results.

If either technique alone were sufficient there would be no reason to combine the two. Thus each must provide some benefit to the other. The contribution of analytical learning to empirical learning is that it provides a general method for incorporating domain knowledge into empirical learning; version spaces are smaller than they would be without the knowledge. From a second perspective, the combination uses empirical learning to permit utilizing weaker forms of knowledge than pure analytical learning would ordinarily be able to use. The combination operates like empirical learning given no knowledge, but can utilize knowledge when provided, and thus exhibits behavior along a spectrum from knowledge-free to knowledge-rich learning.

1.3   Reader's Guide

The generalized version-space framework is first presented in Chapter 2, including details of the incremental version-space merging method. The next four chapters describe different learning tasks solved within the generalized framework using incremental version-space merging. Chapter 3 simply demonstrates that the functionality of the original version-space approach is maintained by the new, generalized approach. The chapter describes the use of incremental version-space merging to emulate the candidate-elimination algorithm, and also extends it to deal with *ambiguous instances*, when instances are not fully identified (such as when the color attribute of some instance is known to be either brown or black without knowing which). Chapter 4 describes the second major contribution of this work, learning from data with bounded inconsistency, the subcase of learning from inconsistent data solved within the framework. This is followed in Chapter 5 by the third major contribution of this work, using incremental version-space merging to combine empirical and analytical learning. Chapter 6 describes how a second learning system can generate the individual version spaces used by incremental version-space merging. A discussion of general computational issues for incremental version-space merging is presented in Chapter 7. The theory underlying the general version-space framework, including conditions of applicability of the approach and an analysis of the correctness of the algorithms involved, is presented in Chapter 8. Chapter 9 concludes the book with a review of major points and an analysis of general issues raised by this work.

Chapter 2

Incremental Version-Space Merging

This chapter describes the generalized version-space approach, as well as *incremental version-space merging*, the incremental learning method developed as part of the framework. The chapter begins with a description of the new, generalized form of version spaces. This is followed by a description of *version-space merging*, an algorithm for intersecting two version spaces in boundary-set notation. The chapter concludes with a description of its use in incremental version-space merging.

2.1 Generalizing Version Spaces

As stated in the preceding chapter, there were two principal insights in Mitchell's original form of version spaces: maintaining a set of candidate concept definitions, and representing the set efficiently by only saving the most specific and most general definitions in the set. These *boundary sets* delimit the original set of candidate concept definitions.

The unfortunate shortcoming of Mitchell's approach was that the set of candidate concept definitions must reflect strict consistency with data. Given some set of training data, only those concept definitions that correctly classify all instances are considered. If no such definition exists, the version space is empty.

9

This work generalizes Mitchell's approach by maintaining his two insights, but removing the assumption of strict consistency with data. A version space is still a set of concept definitions that can be efficiently represented by the set's minimal and maximal elements; however, the method of determining the set is left unspecified, to be determined as appropriate for the given learning task. The key idea is that the learning task should determine the significance of each piece of information, and in particular, which concept definitions to include in the version space given the information. Each piece of information (such as a training instance and its classification) imposes some constraint on which concept definitions may be considered, and thus can be viewed as specifying some set of legal concept definitions. If this set can be represented with boundary sets, it is a version space.

2.2 Version-Space Merging

Not only did the original definition of version spaces assume strict consistency with data—the associated incremental learning method, the candidate-elimination algorithm, did so as well. It eliminates from the version space all concept definitions that are not consistent with a new instance. This work proposes a new incremental learning algorithm for version spaces that removes the assumption of strict consistency with data. It is based on version-space intersection.

Given two version spaces based on different sets of information (about the same concept), the *version-space merging* algorithm will find their intersection, the version space for the combined information, using only boundary-set representations. This is pictured in Figure 2.1. Given version space VS_1 with boundary sets S_1 and G_1, and VS_2 with boundary sets S_2 and G_2, the version-space merging algorithm finds the boundary sets $S_{1 \cap 2}$ and $G_{1 \cap 2}$ for their intersection, $VS_1 \cap VS_2$ (labeled $VS_{1 \cap 2}$). It does so in a two-step process. In the first step $S_{1 \cap 2}$ is assigned the set of minimal generalizations of pairs from S_1 and S_2, and $G_{1 \cap 2}$ is assigned the maximal specializations of pairs from G_1 and G_2. In the second step the process removes overly general elements from $S_{1 \cap 2}$ and overly specific elements from $G_{1 \cap 2}$. In more detail:[1]

---

[1]Mitchell (1978) provides an equivalent version-space intersection algorithm.

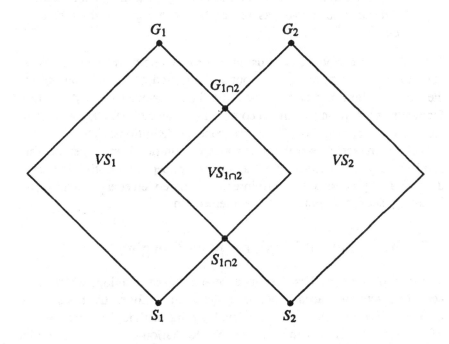

Figure 2.1. Version-Space Merging.

1. For each pair of elements s_1 in S_1 and s_2 in S_2 generate their most specific common generalizations. Assign to $S_{1 \cap 2}$ the union of all such most specific common generalizations of pairs of elements from the two original S-sets. Similarly, generate the set of all most general common specializations of elements of the two G-sets G_1 and G_2 for the new G-set $G_{1 \cap 2}$.

2. Remove from $S_{1 \cap 2}$ those elements that are not more specific than some element from G_1 and some element from G_2. Also remove those elements more general than some other element of $S_{1 \cap 2}$ (generated from a different pair from S_1 and S_2). Similarly remove from

$G_{1\cap2}$ those elements that are not more general than some element from each of S_1 and S_2, as well as those more specific than any other element of $G_{1\cap2}$.

The only information a user must give for this version-space merging algorithm to work is information about the concept description language and the partial order imposed by generality. The user must specify a method for determining the most general common specializations and most specific common generalizations of any two concept definitions. The user must also define the test of whether one concept definition is more general than another. Given this information about the concept description language, the two-step process above will intersect two version spaces, yielding the boundary-set representation of the intersection.

2.3   Incremental Version-Space Merging

The previous section has described version-space merging, which intersects two version spaces in boundary-set form. It forms the basis for *incremental version-space merging*, the learning method developed as part of this work. As each new piece of information—usually a classified instance—is obtained by the learning system, the set of concept definitions deemed relevant are obtained and intersected with the version space generated from past information. The resulting version space reflects all the past information plus the new item.

A learning session begins with an initial version space that contains all concept definitions in the language. This is represented by boundary sets with the S-set containing the empty concept—the concept that says nothing is an example of the concept—and the G-set containing the universal concept—the concept that says everything is an example of the concept. Incremental learning takes place by forming the version space of concept definitions to be considered for a single piece of information and merging it with the version space for past data. This is pictured in Figure 2.2. As each new piece of information is obtained its version space is formed (VS_I) and intersected with the version space for past data (VS_n) to yield a new version space (VS_{n+1}), which will itself be intersected with the version space for the next piece of information.

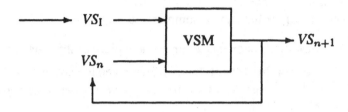

Figure 2.2. Incremental Version-Space Merging.

Use of incremental version-space merging requires a specification by the user of how individual version spaces should be formed. The key insight from which the generality of incremental version-space merging arises is that the specific learning task should define how each piece of information is to be interpreted, and hence how individual version spaces should be formed. The original version-space approach assumed strict consistency with data. For incremental version-space merging, if strict consistency with instances is desired, this must be explicitly specified in how instance version spaces should be formed, namely forming the version space of concept definitions that correctly classify the given instance. Using strict consistency with data to form version spaces results in an emulation of Mitchell's candidate-elimination algorithm, an application of incremental version-space merging discussed in Chapter 3.

However, other methods for forming individual version spaces can also be considered, when strict consistency is not appropriate for the particular learning task. As another example, Chapter 4 describes how some forms of inconsistent data can be handled by including in individual version spaces concept definitions that, although not necessarily consistent with an instance, are at least somewhat reasonable to consider. As a further example, using explanation-based learning to form instance version spaces provides a way to integrate domain knowledge into the learning process. This is discussed further in Chapter 5. Altogether four different learning tasks will be solved using incremental version-space merging.

The general algorithm can be summarized as:

1. Form the version space for the new piece of information.

2. Intersect this version space with the version space generated from past information using the *version-space merging* algorithm.

3. Return to the first step for the next piece of information.

The algorithm thus requires two things from its user: a specification of how version spaces should be formed for each piece of information for Step 1, and information about the concept description language for use by the version-space merging algorithm in Step 2. Both depend on the particular learning task at hand.

Chapter 3

The Candidate-Elimination Algorithm: Emulation and Extensions

This chapter describes how the original version space approach (assuming strict consistency with data) is subsumed by the generalized approach, and in particular, how the candidate-elimination algorithm can be accomplished with incremental version-space merging. This serves as the first test of the generality of incremental version-space merging—that it maintains the functionality of the original version-space approach.

The key idea for emulating the candidate-elimination algorithm is to form the version space of concept definitions strictly consistent with each individual instance and intersect these version spaces with incremental version-space merging. The results after each incremental intersection are the same as those after each step of the candidate-elimination algorithm. The chapter includes an extension to the approach that handles ambiguous data, made possible through the generality of the incremental version-space merging approach.

A hypothetical learning scenario that will be used as an example throughout the chapter is first presented. This is followed by a brief review of the candidate-elimination algorithm. The details of the incremental version-space merging emulation of the candidate-elimination algorithm are then presented, followed by a proof of its equivalence to the candidate-elimination algorithm. The chapter concludes with a description of how ambiguous data can be handled by the new approach.

3.1   Learning Example

The following problem of forming generalizations from classified examples will serve as an example throughout this chapter. Consider a robot manipulating objects on an assembly line. Occasionally it is unable to grasp an object. The learning task is to form rules that will allow the robot to predict when an object is graspable. To make the example simple, the only features of objects that the robot can identify, and hence the only features that may appear in the learned rules, are shape and size. An object may be shaped like a cube, pyramid, octahedron, or sphere, and may have large or small size. Further structure to the shape attribute may be imposed by including in the robot's vocabulary the term "polyhedron" for cubes, pyramids, and octahedra. The generalization hierarchies that result are shown in Figure 3.1. Concept definitions take the form

```
Size(X,small)  ∧ Shape(X,polyhedron)
    → Graspable(X),
```

which will be abbreviated to "[small, polyhedron]." The language is assumed to be sufficient for expressing the desired concept, and the data are assumed to be consistent.

3.2   The Candidate-Elimination Algorithm

This section briefly reviews the details of the candidate-elimination algorithm, and describes its use on the task of learning when an object is graspable. The process begins with the S-set containing the first instance, which must always be positive. This is necessary because the candidate-elimination algorithm assumes that the language for describing instances is a subset of the concept description language—that is, for each instance, there is a concept definition whose extension is only that instance (Dietterich *et al.* (1982) call this the *single-representation trick*). When this

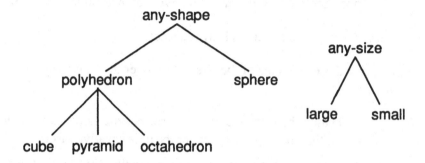

Figure 3.1. Generalization Hierarchies.

is true, the most specific concept definition consistent with the instance (which is what the S-set should contain) is the one that says that only the instance is positive. The G-set contains the universal concept that says everything is positive, since it is the most general concept that includes the positive instance.

Given a new instance, some of the concept definitions in the version space may not classify it correctly. The candidate-elimination algorithm manipulates the boundary-set representation of a version space to create boundary sets that represent a new version space consistent with all the previous instances plus the new one. This is done in a two-step process. If the instance is positive,

1. Remove those elements of the G-set that do not cover the new positive instance.

2. (a) Generalize the elements of the S-set as little as possible (if at all) so that they cover the new positive instance.

   (b) Remove from the S-set those elements that are not most specific (i.e., remove those more general than some other new S-set element). Also remove those concept definitions that are no longer covered by some element of the G-set (i.e., remove those generalizations that now cover some negative instance).

The process for negative instances is symmetric:

1. Remove those elements of the S-set that cover the new negative instance.

2. (a) Specialize the elements of the G-set as little as possible (if at all) so that they no longer cover the new negative instance.

   (b) Remove from the G-set those elements that are not most general and those that no longer cover some element of the S-set.

The concept definition is determined when the version space has only one element, which in the boundary set representation is when the S- and G-sets have the same single element.

As an example of how the candidate-elimination algorithm processes data, consider the following sequence of instances in the robot grasping task. The first object the robot tests is graspable, and is thus a positive example of the target concept. It is a small cube, and hence the initial version space has boundary sets $S=\{[\text{small, cube}]\}$ and $G=\{[\text{any-size, any-shape}]\}$. The second object on the assembly line cannot be grasped, so is a negative instance. It is a small sphere, yielding new boundary sets $S=\{[\text{small, cube}]\}$ and $G=\{[\text{any-size, polyhedron}]\}$—the only way to specialize the G-set to exclude the new instance but still cover the S-set element is to move down the generalization hierarchy for shape from any-shape to polyhedron. A further negative instance, a large octahedron, prunes the version space yet more, to $S=\{[\text{small, cube}]\}$ and $G=\{[\text{any-size, cube}]; [\text{small, polyhedron}]\}$. The new G-set now has two elements since there are two ways to specialize the old G-set to exclude the new instance but still cover the S-set element. After a final, positive instance that is a small pyramid, the boundary sets become $S=G=\{[\text{small, polyhedron}]\}$, yielding the final generalization that all small polyhedral objects are graspable. The processing done by the learning algorithm is summarized in Table 3.1. It gives the S- and G-sets after each instance is processed.

Example	S	G
1. [small, cube] +	{[small, cube]}	{[any-size, any-shape]}
2. [small, sphere] −	{[small, cube]}	{[any-size, polyhedron]}
3. [large, octahedron] −	{[small, cube]}	{[any-size, cube]; [small, polyhedron]}
4. [small, pyramid] +	{[small, polyhedron]}	{[small, polyhedron]}

Table 3.1. Learning Example.

3.3 Candidate-Elimination Algorithm Emulation

The preceding section gives an example of the use of the original candidate-elimination algorithm. This section describes how the functionality of the candidate-elimination algorithm can be emulated by incremental version-space merging. The simple idea is that, as each new training instance is obtained, the set of concept definitions that correctly classify the single instance is formed. This version space is then intersected with the version space generated from prior data, forming a new version space containing the concept definitions consistent with all past data plus the new instance.

Implementing the candidate-elimination algorithm with incremental version-space merging in this manner requires forming the version space of concept definitions that correctly classify a single instance in boundary-set representation. This is done as follows. If the training instance is a positive example, its S-set is set to the most specific elements in the language that include the instance. When the single-representation trick holds, the S-set contains the instance as its sole element. When it does not hold, the learning-task-specific method that generates instance version spaces must determine the set of most specific concept definitions in the language that cover the instance. The new G-set contains the single, universal concept that says that everything is an example of the concept. If the training instance is a negative example, its S-set is taken to be the single, empty concept that says that nothing is an example of the concept, and its G-set is the set of minimal specializations of the universal concept that don't cover the instance. This forms the boundary-set representation of the version space of concept definitions consistent with a single training instance. The computational complexity of this process is discussed in Chapter 7; for conjunctive languages the expected size of the resulting G-set grows linearly in the number of features.

The candidate-elimination algorithm as implemented by incremental version-space merging initially starts with the full version space—the S-set containing the empty concept and the G-set containing the universal concept. Each successive instance is converted into a version space as just described and is merged with the version space for past instances. This process continues until a version space with a single element is obtained. Note that, in contrast to the candidate-elimination algorithm, this emulation allows the first instance to be negative, and furthermore does not assume the single-representation trick.

The emulation can be summarized as follows:

1. Form the version space of all concept definitions consistent with an individual instance.

2. Intersect this new version space with the version space for past data to generate a new version space.

3. Return to Step 1 for the next instance.

Note that this merely instantiates the general incremental version-space merging algorithm specified in Chapter 2, specifying how individual version spaces are formed in Step 1.

To demonstrate this incremental version-space merging implementation of the candidate-elimination algorithm, the robot learning task presented in Section 3.1 will again be used. The initial version space has boundary sets $S=\{\emptyset\}$ and $G=\{[\text{any-size, any-shape}]\}$ (where $\emptyset$ represents the empty concept that says nothing is an example of the target concept). The version space for the first positive instance, a small cube, has the boundary sets $S=\{[\text{small, cube}]\}$ and $G=\{[\text{any-size, any-shape}]\}$ (Step 1 of the incremental version-space merging algorithm), and when merged with the initial version space simply returns the instance version space (Step 2). This is obtained using the version-space merging algorithm (Section 2.2): in its first step the most specific common generalizations of pairs from the two original S-sets are formed—here it is the most specific common generalizations of ∅ and [small, cube]: {[small, cube]}; the second step prunes away those that are not minimal and those not covered by elements of the two original G-sets, but here nothing need be pruned. Similarly, for the new G-set the most general common specialization of [any-size, any-shape] and [any-size, any-shape] is {[any-size, any-shape]}, and nothing need be pruned.

The version space for the second, negative example, a small sphere, is defined by S={∅} and G={[large, any-shape]; [any-size, polyhedron]}—nothing more general excludes the negative instance. When merged with the previous version space, the new boundary sets are S={[small, cube]} and G={[any-size, polyhedron]}. This is obtained by taking for the new S-set the most specific common generalizations of [small, cube] and ∅ that are more specific than [any-size, any-shape] and one of [large, any-shape] and [any-size, polyhedron]—i.e., covered by elements of the two original G-sets. This simply yields {[small, cube]}. For the new G-set the most general common specializations of [any-size, any-shape] and [large, any-shape]—{[large, any-shape]}—and the most general common specializations of [any-size, any-shape] and [any-size, polyhedron]—{[any-size, polyhedron]}—are taken for the new G-set, but [large, any-shape] must be pruned since it is not more general than an element of one of the original S-set elements, [small, cube].

The third, negative example, a large octahedron, has boundary sets S={∅} and G={[small, any-shape]; [any-size, sphere]; [any-size, cube]; [any-size, pyramid]}. Merging this with the preceding boundary sets yields S={[small, cube]} and G={[any-size, cube]; [small, polyhedron]}. Finally, the last, positive instance, a small pyramid, has boundary sets S={[small, pyramid]} and G={[any-size, any-shape]}, resulting in the final version space S=G={[small, polyhedron]}. Tables 3.2 and 3.3 summarize the processing done by the emulation. Table 3.2 gives the boundary sets for the version space generated for each instance (Step 1 of each iteration of incremental version-space merging). Table 3.3 gives the boundary sets obtained by intersecting the instance version spaces (Step 2 of each iteration). Note that at each step the version space after merging (Table 3.3) is the same as that produced by the candidate-elimination algorithm (Table 3.1).

Example	Instance S	Instance G
1. [small, cube] +	{[small, cube]}	{[any-size, any-shape]}
2. [small, sphere] −	{∅}	{[large, any-shape]; [any-size, polyhedron]}
3. [large, octahedron] −	{∅}	{[small, any-shape]; [any-size, sphere]; [any-size, cube]; [any-size, pyramid]}
4. [small, pyramid] +	{[small, pyramid]}	{[any-size, any-shape]}

Table 3.2. Emulation Example: Instance Boundary Sets.

Example	Resulting S	Resulting G
Initial boundary sets:	{∅}	{[any-size, any-shape]}
1. [small, cube] +	{[small, cube]}	{[any-size, any-shape]}
2. [small, sphere] −	{[small, cube]}	{[any-size, polyhedron]}
3. [large, octahedron] −	{[small, cube]}	{[any-size, cube]; [small, polyhedron]}
4. [small, pyramid] +	{[small, polyhedron]}	{[small, polyhedron]}

Table 3.3. Emulation Example: Resulting Boundary Sets.

3.4   Formal Proof of Equivalence

The preceding emulation of the candidate-elimination algorithm can be shown equivalent to the original candidate-elimination algorithm. Mitchell has already shown that the version space generated by the candidate-elimination algorithm after each instance contains all and only those concept definitions consistent with all the data processed to that point (Mitchell, 1978). To demonstrate the equivalence of the incremental version-space merging emulation of the candidate-elimination algorithm it is merely necessary to show that this is also true of the emulation.

Theorem 3.1: *The version space generated by the incremental version-space merging emulation of the candidate-elimination algorithm after each instance contains all and only those concept definitions consistent with all the data processed to that point.*

Proof: The proof utilizes the observation that if all the concept definitions in a version space are consistent with a set of data, then the result of intersecting it with any other version space yields a set of concept definitions all of whose members are consistent with the set of data. This is true because the result of an intersection yields a subset of the original set. If all of the original elements are consistent with the data, then so, too, is the subset obtained by intersection.

The proof is done by induction on n, the number of instances processed. The base case is simple. Since the version space given to incremental version-space merging is the set of all concepts consistent with a single instance, the theorem is trivially true for the base case of $n = 1$.

The induction step for $n = k + 1$ instances (assuming the theorem is true for $n \leq k$) begins by noting that one of the two inputs to the emulation contains the set of all concepts consistent with past data (due to the inductive hypothesis), and the other contains the set of all concepts consistent with the new instance. Thus by the observation above the resulting intersection is consistent with all past data plus the new instance. Furthermore there are no other concepts consistent with all past data plus the new instance, since if such a concept did exist, it would be in each of the two version spaces given to the intersection algorithm, and thus should appear in the intersection. □

3.5 Ambiguous Training Data

Section 3.3 described how incremental version-space merging can be used to emulate the candidate-elimination algorithm. However, ambiguous data can also be handled by the technique. When an instance is not uniquely identified, it is said to be *ambiguous*. For example, only knowing a range for a person's height or age is a form of ambiguous data. More extreme examples are when data are provided at too general a level (such as only knowing that someone is tall), or when attributes are totally missing. The incremental version-space merging emulation of the candidate-elimination algorithm provides a mechanism for doing concept learning even when given ambiguous data. The basic idea is to form the version space of concept definitions for ambiguous data by identifying the set of all concept definitions consistent with any potential identity for the ambiguous instance.

The basic approach still holds—to find the version space of all concept definitions consistent with an instance. When a training instance is ambiguous its version space should include concept definitions consistent with any possible interpretation of the instance. For example, if a positive instance is known to be small and either an octahedron or a cube, its version space should contain all concept definitions that include small octahedra plus all concept definitions that include small cubes. This version space can be viewed as the union of two version spaces, one for small octahedra, and the other for small cubes. If the shape is only known to be polyhedral, its version space contains all concept definitions consistent with cube, octahedron, or pyramid.

Incremental version-space merging simply merges the version space for a new instance with the version space for past instances. If an instance is unambiguous, its version space contains all concept definitions consistent with the instance. However, if the new instance is ambiguous, its version space contains all concept definitions consistent with any single possibility for the instance.

Defining a version space requires defining the contents of its boundary sets. For ambiguous training data this is done by setting the boundary sets to the most specific and general concept definitions consistent with some possibility for the training instance. If the instance is a positive example, the S-set contains the most specific concept definitions that include at least one possible identity for the ambiguous instance. If the single-representation trick holds the S-set contains the set of all instances that the training instance might truly be. The G-set contains the universal concept that matches everything. If the instance is negative the S-set contains the empty concept that matches nothing and the G-set contains the minimal specializations of the universal concept that do not include *one* of the possibilities for the uncertain data. The computational complexity of this process is discussed in Chapter 7.

For example, given the positive training instance that is small and either octahedron or cube, the version space must contain all concept definitions consistent with at least one of the possibilities. The G-set would contain the universal concept that matches everything, and the S-set would contain two elements: [small, octahedron] and [small, cube]. One of the two *must* be a positive example, and this S-set bounds the version space of all concept definitions consistent with the possibilities. They are the most specific concept definitions consistent with some possibility for the training instance.

Note that this cannot be handled through the use of internal disjunction (Michalski, 1983). An example of an internal disjunction would be the concept definition [small, octahedron∨cube]. This says that small objects that are either octahedra or cubes will be positive. Both small octahedra *and* small cubes are included as positive by it. An ambiguous instance, on the other hand, cannot guarantee that both will be positive; it may be that only small cubes are positive, whereas the internal disjunction would errantly include small octahedra. A correct solution to handling ambiguous data must not rule out concept definitions whose extension only includes one of the possible identities of an ambiguous instance.

The algorithm can thus be summarized as follows:

1. (a) Form the set of all instances the given instance might be.

   (b) Form the version space of all concept definitions consistent with any individual instance in this set.

2. Intersect the version space with the version space for past data to obtain a new version space.

3. Return to Step 1 for the next instance.

Again, this is just the algorithm of Chapter 2 with a new specification of how individual version spaces are formed.

To demonstrate such handling of ambiguous data, the learning task of Section 3.1 is again used. If the first, positive instance were known to be small and either cube or octahedron, the instance version space would have boundary sets $S=\{[small, cube]; [small,$

octahedron]} and $G=\{$[any-size, any-shape]}. After the second instance (a small sphere, negative example) is processed, the resulting boundary sets are $S=\{$[small, cube]; [small, octahedron]} and $G=\{$[any-size,
polyhedron]}. The third instance (a large octahedron, negative example) results in $S=\{$[small, cube]; [small, octahedron]} and $G=\{$[any-
size, cube]; [small, polyhedron]}. It takes the final instance (a small
pyramid, positive example) to finally make the version space converge to
$S=G=\{$[small, polyhedron]}. The processing of the incremental version-
space merging emulation of the candidate-elimination algorithm in this
case is summarized in Tables 3.4 and 3.5. Table 3.4 gives the instance
version spaces, and Table 3.5 gives the resulting version spaces after incremental version-space merging.

Example	Instance S	Instance G

1. [small, cube];
    [small, octahedron] +
	{[small, cube];
	  [small, octahedron]}
		{[any-size, any-shape]}

2. [small, sphere] −	{∅}	{[large, any-shape]; [any-size, polyhedron]}

3. [large, octahedron] −	{∅}	{[small, any-shape];
		  [any-size, sphere];
		  [any-size, cube];
		  [any-size, pyramid]}

4. [small, pyramid] +	{[small, pyramid]}	{[any-size, any-shape]}

Table 3.4. Ambiguous Data Example: Instance Boundary Sets.

3.6 Summary

This chapter has shown how the original applications of version spaces
with the candidate-elimination algorithm can be accomplished using incremental version-space merging. The key idea is to form the version space of
concept definitions strictly consistent with each instance and incrementally
intersect these version spaces using the incremental version-space merging algorithm. The emulation of the candidate-elimination algorithm with

Example	Resulting S	Resulting G
Initial boundary sets:	{∅}	{[any-size, any-shape]}
1. [small, cube]; [small, octahedron] +	{[small, cube]; [small, octahedron]}	{[any-size, any-shape]}
2. [small, sphere] −	{[small, cube]; [small, octahedron]}	{[any-size, polyhedron]}
3. [large, octahedron] −	{[small, cube]; [small, octahedron]}	{[any-size, cube]; [small, polyhedron]}
4. [small, pyramid] +	{[small, polyhedron]}	{[small, polyhedron]}

Table 3.5. Ambiguous Data Example: Resulting Boundary Sets.

incremental version-space merging removes the necessity of the single-representation trick, as well as the need for the first instance to be positive. The chapter furthermore demonstrates how ambiguous data can be used in learning, by forming the version space of concept definitions consistent with any possible instance the ambiguous instance might be. This approach to ambiguous data forms the basis for learning from inconsistent data that is presented in the next chapter.

Chapter 4

Learning from Data with Bounded Inconsistency

When no single concept definition in the description language can distinguish between all the positive examples and all the negative examples, the data are said to be *inconsistent* with respect to the concept description language. In such cases no learner will be able to find a description classifying all instances correctly. In general, learning systems must generate reasonable results even when there is no concept definition consistent with all the data.

This chapter describes the application of incremental version-space merging to learning from inconsistent data. The problem pure version-space approaches have with inconsistent data is that some misclassified instance causes the desired concept definition to be removed from consideration. Mitchell suggested a solution to this problem by maintaining in parallel version spaces based on different subsets of the data. The principal difficulty with his approach is that this is a very costly procedure in terms of both time and space. Rather than updating single version spaces, many version spaces must be updated with each instance. Although interesting for theoretical considerations, practical considerations make it unacceptable for general use.

The technique presented here uses a different approach. Rather than keeping all concept definitions strictly consistent with the observed data,

29

the approach described here is more conservative. It keeps all concept definitions consistent with either the instance or some nearby instance. The version space thus contains all concept definitions that are *reasonable* to consider given the data thus far. A larger number of concept definitions are kept in consideration to decrease the chance of removing the desired one.

4.1   Bounded Inconsistency

The approach taken here to learning from inconsistent data foregoes a solution to the full problem, and instead solves a subcase of the problem for one particular class of inconsistency that can be exploited in learning. The underlying assumption for this class of inconsistency is that some small perturbation to the description of any bad instance will result in a good instance. When this is true the data are said to have *bounded inconsistency*. Whenever an instance is misclassified with respect to the desired final concept definition, some nearby instance description has the original instance's classification.

Figure 4.1 shows a simple way to view this. Concepts (such as C) divide the set of instances (I) into positives and negatives. I_1^+ is an example of a representative positive example. It is correctly classified with respect to the desired concept C. Similarly, I_2^- is a correctly classified representative negative example. I_3^+ however is incorrectly classified as positive even though the desired concept would label it negative. However, a neighboring instance description, I'^+_3, is near it across the border, and is correctly classified. Similarly for the incorrectly classified negative instance I_4^- and its neighbor I'^-_4. Roughly speaking, if misclassifications only occur near the desired concept's boundary, the data have bounded inconsistency.

For example, if instances are described by conjunctions of features whose values are determined by measuring devices in the real world, and the measuring devices are known to only be accurate within some tolerance, bounded inconsistency can occur. Consider an instance that is classified as positive, with a feature whose value is 5.0 (obtained by the real-world measuring device). If the tolerance on the measurement of the feature's value is 0.1, the instance could really have been one with feature value 4.9. If the "true" positive instance were 4.9, and the instance that

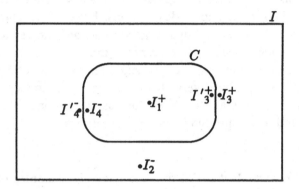

Figure 4.1. Pictorial Representation of Bounded Inconsistency.

really has value 5.0 would have been negative, a misclassification error has occurred. If the tolerance information is correct, for every incorrect instance there is a neighboring correct instance description, all of whose feature values are no more than the tolerance away from the original instance's value for that feature. This is an example of bounded inconsistency.

4.2 The Approach

Informally, the approach taken here for learning from inconsistent data treats all instances as ambiguous, as discussed in the preceding chapter. Rather than forming the space of all concept definitions consistent with the instance, the space of all concept definitions consistent with the instance or some instance description not too distant from the given one is formed (where "not too distant" is defined as appropriate for the particular learning task). The approach handles cases of inconsistent data in which each non-representative or misclassified instance has at least one nearby description that has the original instance's classification as its correct classification.

All instances are treated as capable of being any instance within some region of neighboring instances descriptions. For each instance the set of neighboring instance descriptions is determined, and the version space of concept definitions to be considered contains those concept definitions consistent with the instance or one of its neighbors. The net effect is that all instances are "blurred," and version spaces contain all concept definitions that generate a correct classification for at least one instance in each "blur".

The general technique can be viewed as follows:

Given:

- *Training Data*: Positive and negative examples of the concept to be identified.
- *Definition of Nearby*: A method that determines all instances near a given instance.
- *Concept Description Language*: A language in which the final concept definition must be expressed.

Determine:

- A set of concept definitions in the concept description language consistent with the data or nearby neighbors of the data.

The method proceeds as follows:

1. (a) Determine the set of instances near a given instance.
   (b) Form the version space of all concept definitions consistent with some instance in this set.
2. Intersect this version space with the version space generated from all past data.
3. Return to the first step for the next instance.

If an instance is positive the version space of all concept definitions consistent with some instance in the set of neighboring instances has as an S-set the set of most specific concept definitions that cover at least one of the instances, and as a G-set the universal concept that includes everything. If the single-representation trick holds (i.e., for each instance there is a concept definition whose extension only contains that instance), the S-set contains the set of neighboring instances themselves. If an instance is negative the S-set contains the empty concept that includes nothing and the G-set contains all minimal specializations of the universal concept that excludes the instance or one of its neighbors. The computational complexity of determining this latter set is discussed in Chapter 7; for conjunctive languages the cardinality of the set increases linearly in the number of features used in the language.

4.3 Searching the Version Space

Ideally the result of this learning process would be a singleton version space containing the desired concept definition. However, if not given enough data the final version space will have more than one concept definition. This also happens if the definition of nearby is too generous, since it will allow too many concept definitions into the version space, and no set of instances will permit convergence to a single concept definition. The definition of nearby should be generous enough to guarantee that the desired concept definition is never thrown out by any instance, but not too generous to include too many things (or in the worst case, everything).

In addition, often it will take too long to wait for enough instances to lead to convergence to a single concept definition. As each instance throws away candidate concept definitions, the version space gets smaller and smaller. As the version space decreases in size, the probability that a randomly chosen instance will make a difference—will be able to remove candidate concept definitions—becomes smaller and smaller. The more data processed, the longer the wait for another useful instance. Therefore it will sometimes be desirable due to time considerations to use the small but nonsingleton version space (before converging to a single concept) to determine a usable result for learning.

Thus a situation can arise in which the final version space after processing data has multiple concept definitions. Not all of the remaining concept definitions are equal, though. Some may be more consistent with neighboring instances than given instances—for the concept definition to be consistent with ground data more instances require "blurring." An additional technique is therefore used to obtain a single final concept definition: When a nonsingleton final version space is generated, all candidate concept definitions in the version space are checked for their coverage of the raw, unperturbed data.[1] The concept definition with best coverage is then selected as the final generalization.[2] This is computationally feasible as long as the version space is reasonably small in size.

4.4   Example

To demonstrate this technique Fisher's iris data (Fisher, 1936) is used. The data are inconsistent, and thus the version space of concept definitions strictly consistent with the data is empty.

4.4.1   Problem

The particular problem is that of classifying examples of different kinds of iris flowers into one of three species of irises: setosa, versicolor, and viginica. The goal is to learn three nonoverlapping concept definitions that cover the space of all irises; this requires a slight extension to the version-space approach, which is described in the next subsection. There are 150 instances, 50 for each class; instances are described using four features: sepal width, sepal length, petal width, and petal length. The units for all four are centimeters, measured to the nearest millimeter. For example, one example of setosa had sepal length 4.6cm, sepal width 3.6cm, petal length 1.0cm, and petal width 0.2cm. A full listing of the data appears in Tables 4.1, 4.2, and 4.3.

The concept description language was chosen to be conjunctions of ranges of the form $a \leq x < b$ for each feature, where a and b are limited to

---

[1] This, of course, requires retaining *all* data for this later check of coverage. An alternative strategy would be to retain only a random subset of the data to lessen space requirements.

[2] This is only one possible criterion for selecting a concept definition. Other criteria might consider the amount of "blurring" required to get an instance that matches the concept definition, and select the concept definition that minimizes the sum (or some other function) of the "blurs."

Sepal Length	Sepal Width	Petal Length	Petal Width	Sepal Length	Sepal Width	Petal Length	Petal Width
5.1	3.5	1.4	0.2	5.0	3.0	1.6	0.2
4.9	3.0	1.4	0.2	5.0	3.4	1.6	0.4
4.7	3.2	1.3	0.2	5.2	3.5	1.5	0.2
4.6	3.1	1.5	0.2	5.2	3.4	1.4	0.2
5.0	3.6	1.4	0.2	4.7	3.2	1.6	0.2
5.4	3.9	1.7	0.4	4.8	3.1	1.6	0.2
4.6	3.4	1.4	0.3	5.4	3.4	1.5	0.4
5.0	3.4	1.5	0.2	5.2	4.1	1.5	0.1
4.4	2.9	1.4	0.2	5.5	4.2	1.4	0.2
4.9	3.1	1.5	0.1	4.9	3.1	1.5	0.1
5.4	3.7	1.5	0.2	5.0	3.2	1.2	0.2
4.8	3.4	1.6	0.2	5.5	3.5	1.3	0.2
4.8	3.0	1.4	0.1	4.9	3.1	1.5	0.1
4.3	3.0	1.1	0.1	4.4	3.0	1.3	0.2
5.8	4.0	1.2	0.2	5.1	3.4	1.5	0.2
5.7	4.4	1.5	0.4	5.0	3.5	1.3	0.3
5.4	3.9	1.3	0.4	4.5	2.3	1.3	0.3
5.1	3.5	1.4	0.3	4.4	3.2	1.3	0.2
5.7	3.8	1.7	0.3	5.0	3.5	1.6	0.6
5.1	3.8	1.5	0.3	5.1	3.8	1.9	0.4
5.4	3.4	1.7	0.2	4.8	3.0	1.4	0.3
5.1	3.7	1.5	0.4	5.1	3.8	1.6	0.2
4.6	3.6	1.0	0.2	4.6	3.2	1.4	0.2
5.1	3.3	1.7	0.5	5.3	3.7	1.5	0.2
4.8	3.4	1.9	0.2	5.0	3.3	1.4	0.2

Table 4.1. 50 Positive Examples of Setosa.

multiples of 8 millimeters. An example of a legal concept description has [0.8cm $\leq$ petal length < 2.4cm] and [petal width < 1.6cm]. The range for defining neighboring instances was taken to be 3 millimeters for each feature—that is, as much as 3 millimeters can be added to or subtracted from each feature value for each instance (defining a range of size 6 millimeters centered on each feature value). There is no restriction on the number of features that may be blurred—anywhere from all to none may require blurring.

Note that although this means that each instance could be blurred to

Sepal Length	Sepal Width	Petal Length	Petal Width	Sepal Length	Sepal Width	Petal Length	Petal Width
7.0	3.2	4.7	1.4	6.6	3.0	4.4	1.4
6.4	3.2	4.5	1.5	6.8	2.8	4.8	1.4
6.9	3.1	4.9	1.5	6.7	3.0	5.0	1.7
5.5	2.3	4.0	1.3	6.0	2.9	4.5	1.5
6.5	2.8	4.6	1.5	5.7	2.6	3.5	1.0
5.7	2.8	4.5	1.3	5.5	2.4	3.8	1.1
6.3	3.3	4.7	1.6	5.5	2.4	3.7	1.0
4.9	2.4	3.3	1.0	5.8	2.7	3.9	1.2
6.6	2.9	4.6	1.3	6.0	2.7	5.1	1.6
5.2	2.7	3.9	1.4	5.4	3.0	4.5	1.5
5.0	2.0	3.5	1.0	6.0	3.4	4.5	1.6
5.9	3.0	4.2	1.5	6.7	3.1	4.7	1.5
6.0	2.2	4.0	1.0	6.3	2.3	4.4	1.3
6.1	2.9	4.7	1.4	5.6	3.0	4.1	1.3
5.6	2.9	3.6	1.3	5.5	2.5	4.0	1.3
6.7	3.1	4.4	1.4	5.5	2.6	4.4	1.2
5.6	3.0	4.5	1.5	6.1	3.0	4.6	1.4
5.8	2.7	4.1	1.0	5.8	2.6	4.0	1.2
6.2	2.2	4.5	1.5	5.0	2.3	3.3	1.0
5.6	2.5	3.9	1.1	5.6	2.7	4.2	1.3
5.9	3.2	4.8	1.8	5.7	3.0	4.2	1.2
6.1	2.8	4.0	1.3	5.7	2.9	4.2	1.3
6.3	2.5	4.9	1.5	6.2	2.9	4.3	1.3
6.1	2.8	4.7	1.2	5.1	2.5	3.0	1.1
6.4	2.9	4.3	1.3	5.7	2.8	4.1	1.3

Table 4.2. 50 Positive Examples of Versicolor.

be any of an infinite number of instances within the range specified by the nearness metric (or if values are limited to the nearest millimeter, feature values can be blurred to any of a large number of nearby values), many of the instances are equivalent with respect to the concept description language. Two feature values, although different, can still fall in the same range imposed by the concept description language. Thus only a much smaller set of nearby instances need be considered and enumerated, one from each grouping of values imposed by the concept description language.

Also note that this language does not use the single-representation trick,

Sepal Length	Sepal Width	Petal Length	Petal Width	Sepal Length	Sepal Width	Petal Length	Petal Width
6.3	3.3	6.0	2.5	7.2	3.2	6.0	1.8
5.8	2.7	5.1	1.9	6.2	2.8	4.8	1.8
7.1	3.0	5.9	2.1	6.1	3.0	4.9	1.8
6.3	2.9	5.6	1.8	6.4	2.8	5.6	2.1
6.5	3.0	5.8	2.2	7.2	3.0	5.8	1.6
7.6	3.0	6.6	2.1	7.4	2.8	6.1	1.9
4.9	2.5	4.5	1.7	7.9	3.8	6.4	2.0
7.3	2.9	6.3	1.8	6.4	2.8	5.6	2.2
6.7	2.5	5.8	1.8	6.3	2.8	5.1	1.5
7.2	3.6	6.1	2.5	6.1	2.6	5.6	1.4
6.5	3.2	5.1	2.0	7.7	3.0	6.1	2.3
6.4	2.7	5.3	1.9	6.3	3.4	5.6	2.4
6.8	3.0	5.5	2.1	6.4	3.1	5.5	1.8
5.7	2.5	5.0	2.0	6.0	3.0	4.8	1.8
5.8	2.8	5.1	2.4	6.9	3.1	5.4	2.1
6.4	3.2	5.3	2.3	6.7	3.1	5.6	2.4
6.5	3.0	5.5	1.8	6.9	3.1	5.1	2.3
7.7	3.8	6.7	2.2	5.8	2.7	5.1	1.9
7.7	2.6	6.9	2.3	6.8	3.2	5.9	2.3
6.0	2.2	5.0	1.5	6.7	3.3	5.7	2.5
6.9	3.2	5.7	2.3	6.7	3.0	5.2	2.3
5.6	2.8	4.9	2.0	6.3	2.5	5.0	1.9
7.7	2.8	6.7	2.0	6.5	3.0	5.2	2.0
6.3	2.7	4.9	1.8	6.2	3.4	5.4	2.3
6.7	3.3	5.7	2.1	5.9	3.0	5.1	1.8

Table 4.3. 50 Positive Examples of Setosa.

and its features do not form a tree-structured hierarchy, two properties that are commonly used to guarantee computational tractability. This language does have other properties, however, that allow similar computational guarantees (Chapter 7).

4.4.2 Method

The general approach of Section 4.2 was used to find rules. All neighboring instances for each instance are generated, by perturbing the instance in all ways possible—0.3 is added to and subtracted from each feature value, and the concept definitions consistent with each combination of potential feature values were formed. The union of all these concept definitions forms the version space for individual instances. For example, the positive instance of setosa given earlier (with sepal length 4.6cm, sepal width 3.6cm, petal length 1.0cm, and petal width 0.2cm), has four elements in its S-set. All have [3.2cm $\leq$ sepal width $<$ 4.0cm] and [0.0cm $\leq$ petal width $<$ 0.8cm]. They differ, however, on their restrictions on sepal length and petal length: the different concept definitions correspond to the four different combinations obtainable by choosing one of [4.0cm $\leq$ sepal length $<$ 4.8cm] and [4.8cm $\leq$ sepal length $<$ 5.6cm], and one of [0.0cm $\leq$ petal length $<$ 0.8cm] and [0.8cm $\leq$ petal length $<$ 1.6cm]. The G-set for the instance contains the universal concept that includes everything as positive.

The goal of learning is to form three disjoint concept definitions that cover the space of instances, and this requires two extensions to the technique described above. The first exploits the fact that the learned concept definitions must not overlap. The simple approach would be to take the 100 examples of two of the classes as negative examples for the third class. However, not only must the concept definitions for the third class exclude these instances, they must exclude all instances included by the final concept definition for each of the other two classes. It is not known what the final definitions will be, but it is known that they must be more general than some element of the S-set for its class. That is, whatever the concept definition, it must at least include all instances covered by some most specific concept definition generated from the positive data for that class. In the iris domain the S-set for each class after processing the positive data for that class was always singleton, so the final concept definition for each class must include all examples included by the final S-set element. Therefore, rather than taking the 50 examples of each class as negative data for the other two classes, first only positive data are processed for each class, and the resulting generalization in the S-set is taken as a generalized negative instance for the other two classes, replacing the use of the 100 negative instances with two generalizations that include the negative instances plus additional instances that must also be excluded. Thus, for example, all positive data are processed for the setosa class, and the result in the S-set is taken as a single generalized negative instance for versicolor and viginica. It summarizes the setosa data, as well as additional instances that will also be included by the final definition for setosa.

The second extension is that, since the three concept definitions that are formed must cover the space, many of the more specific definitions for each class can be removed, since no combination of definitions in the version spaces for the other two classes will cover the space of irises. Instead of applying the technique for searching the version space to find the best concept definition (Section 4.3), only the subset of the version space that could lead to class definitions that cover the space of irises is considered. The search then takes place in the cross products of the three much smaller version spaces. Furthermore, selection of a hypothesis in one space allows using it as a generalized negative instance for the other version spaces, so not all triples of concept definitions from the three version spaces need be considered.

4.4.3   Results

Since there is only a fixed amount of data, the learning technique was evaluated by dividing the data into 10 sets of 15 instances, five from each of the three classes. Learning took place by processing nine of the 10 data sets combined and testing on the tenth data set. This was done for each possible group of nine data sets, and the resulting classification rates were averaged across all 10 runs. A typical final result for a run is a rule set that classifies irises with [petal length $<$ 2.4cm] as setosa, irises with [petal length $\geq$ 2.4cm] and [petal width $<$ 1.6cm] as versicolor, and irises with [petal length $\geq$ 2.4cm] and [petal width $\geq$ 1.6cm] as viginica.

The average overall classification rate on the test data (the remaining one-tenth of each batch used for testing) was 97%—on average 97% of the test cases were placed in the proper class. For the setosa class alone the rate was 100%, as the class is separable from the other two. For versicolor alone the rate was 93%, and for viginica 94%. These rates are comparable to those obtained with other techniques: for example, Dasarathy's pattern-recognition approach (1980) obtained 95% accuracy (100% for setosa, 98% for versicolor, and 86% for viginica); Aha and Kibler's noise-tolerant nearest-neighbor method NTgrowth (Aha and Kibler, 1989), also obtained 95% accuracy (100% for setosa, 94% for versicolor, and 91% for viginica); and C4 (Quinlan, 1987), Quinlan's noise-tolerant version of ID3, obtained 94% accuracy (100% for setosa, and 91% for versicolor and viginica).[3] The results are summarized in Table 4.4. NTgrowth and Dasarathy's method are both instance-based; C4 is the only other learning method that can be said to use a concept description language. For example, on one run it generated the decision tree that defines irises with [petal length < 2.5cm] as setosa, irises with [petal length ≥ 2.5cm] and [petal width < 1.8cm] as versicolor, and those remaining ([petal length ≥ 2.5cm] and [petal width ≥ 1.8cm]) as viginica. Note that, unlike this work, C4 decides for itself where attribute values should be divided. The significance of these results is that, despite its added generality, incremental version-space merging is able to do as well as other learning systems specifically developed for learning from inconsistent data.

Learning Algorithm	Setosa	Viginica	Versicolor	Overall
IVSM	100%	93.33%	94.00%	96.67%
Dasarathy	100%	98%	86%	94.67%
NTgrowth	100%	93.50%	91.13%	94.77%
C4	100%	91.07%	90.61%	94.00%

Table 4.4. Predictive Accuracy of Learning Systems.

4.5   Comparison to Related Work

This chapter describes one approach to dealing with inconsistent data in version-space learning. Drastal, Meunuer, and Raatz (Drastal *et al.*, 1989) have proposed a related method that works in cases where only positive data have bounded inconsistency. Their approach is to overfit the inconsistent data, using a learning technique capable of forming multiple disjuncts, some of which only exist to cover anomalous instances. After learning,

---

[3]These latter two results are due to Aha (personal communication).

they remove disjuncts that only cover instances that can be perturbed to fit under one of the other disjuncts, in effect removing the disjunctions that only exist to cover the anomalous data. One benefit of their technique is that it is applied after learning, focusing on only those instances covered by small disjuncts, whereas here all instances must be viewed as potentially anomalous. However, they make the stronger assumption that all such inconsistent data fall into small disjuncts. They furthermore only handle positive data.

As mentioned earlier, Mitchell (1978) presented an alternative approach to learning from inconsistent data with version spaces. The key idea was to maintain in parallel version spaces for various subsets of the data. When no concept definition is consistent with all data, Mitchell's approach considers those concept definitions consistent with all but one instance. As more inconsistency is detected, the system uses version spaces based on smaller and smaller subsets of the data, which the system has been maintaining during learning. The number of boundary sets that need be maintained by this process is linear in the total number of instances to be processed (in the worst case). This is still unacceptably costly. In the iris domain, assuming that at most 10% of the data should be discounted, this would have required updating 30 boundary sets for each instance. Even using the less reasonable assumption that only 4% of the data need be ignored will result in an order of magnitude slow down. Furthermore, Mitchell's approach requires knowing the absolute maximum number of incorrectly classified instances, in contrast to allowing unlimited number of errors as done here (replacing it with a bound on the distance any instance may be from a correct instance). Finally, the boundary sets for Mitchell's approach are much larger than for the noise-free case, since Mitchell modifies the candidate-elimination algorithm S-set updating method to ignore negative data, and similarly positive data are ignored by the modified G-set updating method (this allows the use of a linear number of boundary sets by keeping the boundary sets for multiple version spaces in a single boundary set).

A significant distinction can be made between this work and Mitchell's approach, as well as much other work in learning from inconsistent data (e.g., Michalski & Larson, 1978; Quinlan, 1986). These approaches form concept definitions that perform well but not perfectly on the data, viewing those instances not covered as anomalous. Instances are effectively thrown away, whereas here every instance is viewed as providing useful information, and the final concept definition must be consistent with the instance or one of its neighbors. The approach presented here works on data with bounded inconsistency. Other approaches handle a wider range of inconsistency, but cannot utilize any instances that are just a small ways off from correct; they instead throw out such instances as nonhelpful. Furthermore, unlike other approaches that degenerate as more inconsistency is imposed on the data, the incremental version-space merging approach described in this chapter still succeeds even when all of the data are subject to inconsistency.

To further demonstrate this point a series of runs of the learning method were done on a simple, artificial domain. There are three attributes that take on real values in the range of 0 to 9. The concept description language partitions attributes into three regions: greater than or equal to 0 and less than 3, greater than or equal to 3 and less than 6, and greater than or equal 6 and less than or equal to 9. A concept definition is a conjunction of such ranges over the various attributes. A single preselected concept definition serves as the target of learning.

Data were created by randomly generating some value for each attribute in its legal range (0 to 9). This instance was then classified according to the preselected target concept definition for learning. The identity of each instance is then perturbed by up to one unit—a random number between −1 and 1 is added to the given value of each attribute. This new instance is given the classification of the instance on which it is based. Training data generated in this manner have bounded inconsistency, since any incorrect instance is never more than 1 away from a correct instance on any attribute.

The test runs perturb different percentages of the data, to test the sensitivity of the approach to this factor. The definition of "nearby" used by the learning method defines one instance to be near another if the value of each attribute of the first are within 1 unit of the corresponding value for the second (i.e., the appropriate definition of nearby was selected). All attribute values for a single instance may be perturbed. 80 randomly generated instances were used.

Table 4.5 summarizes the results of the test. The amount of data that was perturbed was allowed to vary from 0% (no data perturbed—data are

%	Correct?
0	Yes
20	Yes
40	Yes
60	Yes
80	Yes
100	Yes

Table 4.5. Correct Concept Identification for Different Amounts of Inconsistency.

consistent) to 100% (all data perturbed). In all cases learning used a definition of "nearby" that added 1 to and subtracted 1 from the value of each attribute. The result of the experiment was that, in all cases, incremental version-space merging (with the additional step of selecting the best classifier from the version space) converged to the target concept definition that was used to generate the data. Unlike most other learning algorithms that degenerate as more noise is introduced to the data, the technique was able to correctly learn the desired concept definition even when all data are perturbed within known bounds. One way to interpret these results is that the approach described in this chapter for learning from data with bounded inconsistency provides a way to use the knowledge that bounded inconsistency exists, which permits successful learning even when all the data are incorrect (within the known bounds).

4.6 Discussion

The general approach described in this chapter is for version spaces to contain all concept definitions consistent with the instance or some neighbor of the instance. The technique requires a method for generating all instances near a given instance, but it does not constrain *a priori* the particular definition of "nearby." For example, in tree-structured description languages one such definition would be that two feature values are in the same subtree: rhombus and square might be close whereas rhombus and oval might not.

However, the approach described here is extremely sensitive to both the concept description language and the definition of "nearby". For a fixed language, if the notion of nearby is too small, the version space will collapse with no consistent concept; if it is too large, each instance will have many neighbors, and instance boundary sets will be quite large, which makes the approach computationally infeasible (Chapter 7). Furthermore, the final version space will likely be too big to search for a best concept after processing the data. Similarly, for a fixed definition of nearby, if the concept description language is too coarse, instances will have no neighbors, whereas if the language is too fine, then instances will have too many neighbors. The choice of language and definition of nearby affects the size of version spaces and the convergence rate for learning (how many instances are required to converge, if it is even possible).

The ideal situation for this approach would be when the definition of nearby is given or otherwise known for the particular domain, as well as when the desired language for concepts is provided. However, it is often the case that one or both are not known, as was the case for the iris domain of the previous section, which required a few iterations before a successful concept description language and definition of nearby was found. The first description language chosen used intervals of size 4 millimeters, rather than 8 as was finally selected. The first definition of nearby considered instances with feature values within 2 millimeters of given feature values as "nearby", but the version space collapsed—no concept definition remained after processing the data—for the versicolor and viginica classes. However, a definition of nearby of 3 millimeters resulted in too many neighbors for each instance, making the process too computationally expensive (the program ran out of memory). Since measurements were only given to the nearest millimeter, there was no intermediate definition of nearby to try. Since adjusting the definition of nearby failed to work, the next step was to adjust the language, and 8 millimeter intervals were chosen. Fortunately the first attempt using the new language with a definition of nearby of 3 millimeters yielded nonempty version spaces of reasonable size. Criteria for selecting appropriate description languages and definitions of nearby is an area for future work.

To further demonstrate this issue a number of runs were made on the artificial learning task of the previous section. In these experiments the concept description language was fixed (using the same language as in the previous chapter) and the definition of nearby (the amount of inconsistency assumed present by the learning method) was varied. 100% of the attribute values were perturbed by up to 1 unit. This set of experiments explores how the definition of nearby affects the size of the final version space and the number of neighbors each instance will have.

The results of these experiments are summarized in Table 4.6. There are three attributes, and altogether there are 216 concept definitions in the language. The different rows correspond to different definitions of nearby—how much is added to or subtracted from each instance. This was varied from 0 to 3—the maximum distance apart the feature values of two instances can be so that the instances are still considered neighbors (column 1 in the table). Note that the real amount of variance imposed on values when generating data was at most 1—no more than 1 was added to or subtracted from the randomly generated value for the feature. The second column summarizes the size of the final version space after all 80 instances have been processed. Note that, while learning is impossible here if the data are assumed consistent, and convergence is possible using the 80 instances if the definition of nearby adds or subtracts only 1 to each value (the actual value used in generating the inconsistent data), as the value for nearby increases to 2 and 3 the final version-space size increases.

Nearby	Average $|VS|$	Average # Neighbors
0	0	1
1	1	3
2	4	6.48
3	38	12.91

Table 4.6. Version Space Size and Number of Neighbors for Different Definitions of "Nearby."

The third column presents the average number of neighbors for each instance. As would be expected, this number increases as the amount by which values may be perturbed increases, and are close to their expected values of 1.0, 3.0 (= $(13/9)^3$), 6.7 (= $(17/9)^3$), and 12.7 (= $(21/9)^3$).

In general, if there are k features, each with m ranges of size w (here k, m, and w are all 3), and the amount of noise is $d \leq w$ (here d ranged from zero to three), the expected number of neighbors (assuming a uniform distribution of values for each feature and indepedence of features) is $(1 + \frac{2d}{w}(1 - \frac{1}{m}))^k$.

As expected, as the definition of nearby grows more generous, the various quantities increase. These results emphasize the need for a sufficiently generous, but not overly generous, definition of nearby. They furthermore suggest a method for automating the selection of an appropriate definition of nearby given a fixed concept description language. The method would begin by assuming consistency, then slowly increase the amount of inconsistency assumed to be present in the data (i.e., increase the generosity of the definition of nearby) until either a nonempty version space is generated or enough time has passed to believe that the approach is not computationally feasible on the given data with the given concept description language.

4.7 Formal Results

As a final topic of discussion, recent theoretical work on concept learning (e.g., (Haussler, 1988)) has developed techniques for analyzing how the quality of results is influenced by the amount of data used in learning. This section gives such an analysis for learning from data with bounded inconsistency.

To do this a number of definitions are necessary. First, the function *Neighbors(x)* gives the set of examples in the instance description language that are near x (for the learning-task specific definition of nearby):

Definition 4.1:

$$Neighbors(x) = \{y \mid y \text{ is near } x\}.$$

Furthermore, since data may have bounded inconsistency, it is necessary to redefine what it means for a concept definition to be consistent with an instance. A concept is consistent with an example if it correctly classifies the example or one of its neighbors:

Definition 4.2: *An instance x is said to be consistent with a concept C (written Consistent(x, C)) if, when x is positive, $\exists p \in Neighbors(x)$ with $p \in C$, and when x is negative, $\exists n \in Neighbors(x)$ with $n \notin C$ (where $p \in C$ means C would have classified p as positive, and $n \notin C$ means C would have classified n as negative).*

The definition of the error of a concept definition h with respect to a desired target concept C is now defined relative to this new notion of consistency—it is the probability that h and C disagree:

Definition 4.3: *Error(h, C) = the probability that for a randomly chosen instance x classified as a positive or negative example of C, it is not the case that Consistent(x, h).*

With these definitions it is possible to map over Lemma 2.2 from Haussler's *A.I. Journal* paper (Haussler, 1988):

Lemma 4.1: *The probability that some element of the version space generated from m examples of C has error greater than ϵ is less than $|H|e^{-\epsilon m}$, where $|H|$ is the number of expressions in the concept description language H used by incremental version-space merging.*

Proof: Assume that some set of hypotheses $h_1, \ldots, h_k$ in the concept description language H have error greater than ϵ with respect to C. This means that the probability that an example of C is consistent with a particular h_i is less than $(1 - \epsilon)$. The probability that h_i is consistent with m independent examples of C is therefore less than $(1 - \epsilon)^m$. Finally, the probability that *some* $h_i \in h_1, \ldots, h_k$ is consistent with m instances is bounded by the sum of their individual probabilities, thus the probability that some h_i with error greater than ϵ (with respect to C) is consistent with m examples of C is less than $k(1 - \epsilon)^m$. Since $k \leq |H|$, and $(1 - \epsilon)^m \leq e^{-\epsilon m}$, the probability of getting some hypothesis with error greater than ϵ consistent with m independent examples of C is less than $|H|e^{-\epsilon m}$. $\square$

A simple corollary of this Lemma says how many examples are necessary to guarantee with high probability that all concept definitions in the version space have low error:

Corollary 4.1: *The probability that all elements of the version space generated from at least*

$$\frac{ln(|H|) + ln(\frac{1}{\delta})}{\epsilon}$$

examples of C will have error less than ϵ is $1 - \delta$.

Proof: Solving $\delta < |H|e^{-\epsilon m}$ for m gives the desired result. $\square$

At first these results may appear somewhat surprising, since they give the same guarantees as Haussler, yet address learning from inconsistent data. The reason for this is that these results use a weaker definition of consistent, and hence use a weaker notion of error, than the traditional definition used by Haussler.

Finally, note that these results do not only apply to the version space approach presented here. Any learning method that generates concept descriptions "consistent" (in the sense of Definition 2) with m examples of some concept C will have these guarantees.

4.8 Summary

This chapter has described an application of incremental version-space merging that learns from data with bounded inconsistency. The central idea is to find concept definitions not necessarily consistent with the training data, but consistent with either the data or nearby data. This results in considering more concept definitions than the version-space approach would ordinarily consider, decreasing the chance that the desired concept definition is removed due to an anomalous instance.

Chapter 5

Combining Empirical and Analytical Learning

There have been two principal approaches to the problem of concept learning. The first, *empirical learning* (also known as *similarity-based learning*), finds concept descriptions that best cover a set of training data without the use of an extensive theory of the domain. The candidate-elimination algorithm is one example of empirical learning. The second approach, *analytical learning* (also known as *explanation-based learning*) (Mitchell *et al.*, 1986; DeJong and Mooney, 1986), finds the weakest preconditions on a knowledge-based analysis of a single instance, forming a generalization that covers all instances that have the same analysis.

The two techniques each have shortcomings. Empirical approaches do not provide general methods for using knowledge in determining the generalization. On the other hand, analytical methods require very strong forms of knowledge. Furthermore, analytical methods do not make inductive leaps. Their results are based on the knowledge that the learning system is given.

These shortcomings have led researchers to propose combining the two techniques, using each approach to address the shortcomings of the other (e.g., Danyluk, 1987; Flann and Dietterich, 1990; Lebowitz, 1986; Mitchell, 1984; and Pazzani, 1988). This chapter presents one such hybrid learning method, implemented using incremental version-space merging. The general idea is to use incremental version-space merging on the results

49

of analytical learning, rather than on the ground data. The combination operates like empirical learning given no knowledge, but can utilize knowledge when provided, and thus exhibits behavior along a spectrum from knowledge-free to knowledge-rich learning. Given an incomplete theory (i.e., it only explains a subset of potential instances), when an explanation exists empirical learning works on the analytically generalized data; when no explanation can be found the learner utilizes the ground data. When there is no domain theory at all the hybrid approach degenerates to look like the candidate-elimination algorithm.

This chapter begins by summarizing the analytical learning method, *explanation-based generalization*, used in this work. The general approach taken to combine it with version spaces is then presented. This is followed by two examples of the use of the technique. The chapter discusses what the combination approach offers that each approach alone does not. The chapter concludes with a discussion of related work.

5.1 Explanation-Based Generalization

Explanation-based generalization (EBG) (Mitchell *et al.*, 1986) proves that a *goal concept* holds for a single positive *training instance*, using a *domain theory* of rules and facts about the goal concept. EBG forms a generalization of the instance, defining the class of instances that are examples with the same proof as the training instance. It does so by finding the weakest preconditions on the proof, restricting such conditions to expressions that satisfy an *operationality criterion* on the merit of the generalization for the problem solver. The version of EBG used in this work is ROE (Hirsh, 1988).

EBG is typically used in one of two ways. The first, exemplified by the now-classic `Safe-To-Stack` and `Cup` examples (Mitchell *et al.*, 1986) and the classical use of chunking in Soar (Laird *et al.*, 1986; Rosenbloom and Laird, 1986), uses EBG to learn specialized rules that are added to the domain theory to improve its speed on special cases. The second use, exemplified by LEAP (Mitchell *et al.*, 1985a) and data-chunking (Rosenbloom *et al.*, 1987), uses EBG to determine specializations of the domain theory that model the training data.

In the former, domain theories are *predictive*: the classification of the instance provides no useful information, since the classification can be determined using the domain theory. The rule that EBG learns is a specialization of the domain theory, and the rule is merely added back to the theory so that a single rule can be used on comparable instances in the future, rather than chaining through a series of rules as would be required in the theory without the results of EBG. The goal of learning is performance improvement, to classify unseen instances more quickly.

In contrast, the domain theories in the second use of EBG are *explanatory*: given a description of an instance, the theory cannot be used to predict its classification, but can be used retrospectively to explain its classification once it is provided. Such theories can explain many things; the goal of learning is to find a specialization of the theory that predicts the observed data without including many additional items explainable by the theory. For example, LEAP (Mitchell *et al.*, 1985a) learns rules for converting logical expressions into gate-level implementations for use by VEXED (Mitchell *et al.*, 1985b), a tool to aid users in circuit design. VEXED begins with an initial set of rules for transforming logical expressions into implementations. At each step the user guides the system from an initial logical expression to a final gate-level implementation by selecting one of the transformation rules at each step of the design process. Occasionally, however, the user wants to make a transformation not covered by an existing rule. In such cases the user instead specifies what the result should be, and LEAP generalizes the transformation using a domain theory with rules about logic (e.g., including DeMorgan's Laws). The domain theory can explain any valid transformation the user *might* make; LEAP ultimately learns a specialization of the theory that includes the rules the user *desires*—it creates a specialization of its theory that models the data. This use of EBG addresses the criticism leveled by Russell and others (e.g., (Russell, 1987; Mitchell *et al.*, 1986; van Harmelen and Bundy, 1988)) that EBG does not require the training instance, since the theory already defines the concept. They only consider the use of EBG with predictive domain theories; however, when used with explanatory theories, EBG *requires* training data, since the goal of learning is to model the data. (Cf. Flann and Dietterich's (1990) *theory-based concept specialization* problem.)

The major shortcoming of EBG is its reliance on the domain theory that is used in explaining training data. EBG can only learn if the desired concept definition is included in the domain theory. The domain theory must be able to explain all correct instances. Furthermore, the assumption has been that when there are multiple explanations, the first explanation found is always correct. More realistic learning systems must be able to handle incomplete theories that cannot explain all cases, and contradictory theories that may allow for more than one explanation, in which each explanation potentially conflicts with the others. The use of incremental version-space merging described in this chapter weakens the dependency of EBG on its domain theory.

5.2   Combining EBG with Incremental Version-Space Merging

The central idea in this work is to apply empirical learning to the results of analytical learning rather than to pure training data. The problem addressed is:

Given:

- *Training Data*: Positive and negative examples of the concept to be identified. Training data are expressed within an instance description language, whose terms are assumed to be operational.

- *Concept Description Language*: A language in which the final concept must be expressed. It is a superset of the instance description language, and is where generalization hierarchies would appear. Constraints on this input are discussed further in Section 5.5.

- *Positive-Data Domain Theory* (optional): A set of rules and facts for proving that an instance is positive. Proofs terminate in elements of the instance description language.

- *Negative-Data Domain Theory* (optional): A set of rules and facts for proving that an instance is negative. Proofs terminate in elements of the instance description language.

Determine:

- A set of concept definitions in the concept description language consistent with the potentially generalized data.

The method processes a sequence of instances as follows, starting with the first instance:

1. (a) If possible, apply EBG to the current instance to generate a generalized instance. Do so for all possible explanations. If no explanation is found, pass along the ground data.

   (b) Form the version space of all concept definitions consistent with the (perhaps generalized) instance. If there are multiple explanations include those concept definitions consistent with any single explanation.

2. Intersect this version space with the version space generated from all past data.

3. Return to the first step for the next instance.

The basic technique is to form the version space of concept definitions consistent with the explanation-based generalization of each instance as it is obtained (rather than the version space of concept definitions consistent with the ground data). The version space for a single training instance reflects the explanation-based generalization of the instance, representing the set of concept definitions consistent with all instances that are explained in the same manner as the given instance. The merging algorithm has the effect of updating the version space with the many examples sharing the same explanation, rather than with the single instance. In this manner irrelevant features of the instances are removed, and learning can converge to a final concept definition using fewer instances.

The combination of incremental version-space merging and EBG also applies to cases of multiple competing explanations, when only one explanation need be correct. In such cases the version space of concept definitions consistent with one or more of the potential results of EBG is formed. EBG is applied to every competing explanation of an instance, each yielding a competing generalization of the instance. The space of candidate generalizations for the single instance contains all concept definitions consistent with *at least one* of the competing generalizations. The final generalization after multiple instances must be consistent with one of them. The situation is similar to that of ambiguous data (Chapter 3), only here it is unknown which *explanation* is correct. Like the earlier treatment of ambiguous data, the version space contains all concept definitions consistent with at least one of the possibilities.

The version space of all concept definitions consistent with at least one explanation-based generalization of the instance is the union of the version spaces of concept definitions consistent with each individual explanation-based generalization. For positive examples this union has as its S boundary set the set of competing explanation-based generalizations,[1] and the G boundary set contains the universal concept. If one result of EBG is more general than another (e.g., one mentions a superset of the training-instance facts mentioned by the other), only the more specific result is kept in the S-set. Over multiple instances these version spaces consistent with the explanation-based generalizations are incrementally intersected to find the space of concept definitions consistent with the generalized data.

The approach is also useful given theories for explaining *negative* data, when the system is provided with a theory capable of explaining why an instance is negative. For example, in search control an example of a state in which an operator should *not* be used is a negative instance, and a theory for explaining why the instance is negative would analyze why the instance is negative—that the operator does not apply, or that it leads to a non-optimal solution. This theory is then used to generalize the negative instance to obtain a generalization covering all instances that are negative for the same

---

[1]This requires an assumption similar to the single-representation trick (Dietterich *et al.*, 1982), namely that all results of EBG are in the concept description language used by empirical learning. This is discussed further in Section 5.5.

reason. Incremental version-space merging then uses this generalized instance by setting the S-set equal to the empty concept that says nothing is an example of the concept, and setting the G-set equal to all minimal specializations of the universal concept that do not cover the generalized negative instance. If there are multiple competing explanations the G-set contains all minimal specializations that do not cover at least one of the potential generalizations obtainable by EBG using one of the explanations.

Note that it is not necessary to have a complete theory capable of explaining (and generalizing) all correct instances for this technique to work. The version space of all concept definitions consistent with plain non-generalized instances—whether negative or positive examples—can always be formed. Instead of using EBG, the version space contains all concept definitions consistent with the instance, rather than its explanation-based generalization. If a theory for only explaining positive instances exists, negative instances can be processed without using EBG. If an incomplete theory exists (i.e., it only explains a subset of potential instances), when an explanation exists the version space for the explanation-based generalization of the instance can be used, otherwise the pure instance version space should be used. When there is no domain theory the learner behaves like the candidate-elimination algorithm. The net result is a learning method capable of exhibiting behavior at various points along the spectrum from knowledge-free to knowledge-rich learning.

5.3 Examples

To illustrate how incremental version-space merging combines empirical and analytical learning, two examples are presented. The first demonstrates how empirical learning generalizes beyond the specific results obtainable with EBG alone. The second demonstrates how empirical learning deals with competing explanations.

5.3.1 Cup Example

The first example of the combination of incremental version-space merging and EBG demonstrates how a definition of Cup can be learned given incomplete knowledge about cups plus examples of cups. It is based on the examples given by Mitchell *et al.* (1986) and Flann and Dietterich (1990).

The following is the domain theory used (written in Prolog notation):

```
cup(X):-holds_liquid(X),can_drink_from(X),
        stable(X).
holds_liquid(X):-pyrex(X).
holds_liquid(X):-china(X).
holds_liquid(X):-aluminum(X).
can_drink_from(X):-liftable(X),open_top(X).
liftable(X):-small(X).
stable(X):-flat_bottom(X).
```

It can recognize and explain some, but not all, cups. The concept description language used for this problem by empirical learning utilizes generalization hierarchies, including the knowledge that pyrex, china, and aluminum are nonporous materials, and that black and brown are dark colors. Note that this information is not present in the domain theory, but is known to be true in general. Empirical learning has many such possible generalizations. The goal for learning is to determine which potential generalizations, such as those mentioning nonporous material, are relevant.

Learning begins with the first, positive example:

```
china(cup1).
small(cup1).
open_top(cup1).
flat_bottom(cup1).
black(cup1).
```

EBG results in the rule

```
cup(X):-china(X),small(X),open_top(X),
        flat_bottom(X).
```

written "[china, small, open, flat, anycolor]" for short. This forms the *S*-set for the version space of the first instance (and the first step of incremental version-space merging), and its *G*-set contains the universal concept [anymaterial, anysize, anytop, anybottom, anycolor]. The second step of incremental version-space merging intersects this with the initial full version space, which gives back this first-instance version space.

Incremental version-space merging then returns to its first step for the next, positive instance, which is:

```
pyrex(cup2).
small(cup2).
open_top(cup2).
flat_bottom(cup2).
brown(cup2).
```

EBG results in the rule

```
cup(X):-pyrex(X),small(X),open_top(X),
         flat_bottom(X).
```

The *S*-set for this instance's version space contains the result of EBG, namely [pyrex, small, open, flat, anycolor], and its *G*-set contains the universal concept. Merging this with the version space for the first iteration yields a version space whose *S*-set contains [nonporous, small, open, flat, anycolor] and whose *G*-set contains the universal concept.

The final instance is a negative example:

```
aluminum(can1).
small(can1).
closed_top(can1).
flat_bottom(can1).
white(can1).
```

For this example the theory of negative data is assumed to include the following rules (among others):

```
not_a_cup(X):-cannot_drink_from(X).
cannot_drink_from(X):-closed_top(X).
```

EBG yields the following rule:

```
not_a_cup(X):-closed_top(X).
```

This is then used to determine the most general concept definitions that exclude this generalized case of not_a_cup, namely [anymaterial, anysize, open, anybottom, anycolor], which forms the G-set of the version space for this third instance. The S-set contains the empty concept.

When this third instance version space is merged with the result of the previous two iterations of incremental version-space merging, the resulting S-set contains [nonporous, small, open, flat, anycolor] and the resulting G-set contains [anymaterial, anysize, open, anybottom, anycolor]. Note that the domain theories have done part of the work, with the color attribute being ignored and only the third attribute being deemed relevant for the negative instance, but empirical learning determining nonporous. Further data would continue refining the version space. However, it is already known that whatever the final rule, it will include small, nonporous, open-topped objects, like Styrofoam cups, which the original theory did not recognize as cups.

This simple domain also demonstrates the point made earlier about the technique degenerating to look like pure empirical learning. Consider the same examples, only without the domain theory present. At each iteration the resulting version space will be exactly the same as would be created by the candidate-elimination algorithm. The final version space would have an S-set containing [nonporous, small, open, flat, darkcolor], and a G-set containing two elements: [anymaterial, anysize, open, anybottom, anycolor] and [anymaterial, anysize, anytop, anybottom, darkcolor]. This version space contains more elements than the corresponding version space from the previous paragraph.

5.3.2   Can_put_on_table Example

As an example of using domain theories with multiple competing explanations, consider the following domain theory for can_put_on_table:

```
can_put_on_table(X):-stable(X),small(X).
can_put_on_table(X):-stable(X),light(X).
stable(X):-flat_bottom(X).
```

It provides two potential explanations for when an object can successfully be placed on a table: the object must be stable, and either small or light.

Given an unclassified instance, the theory cannot be used to predict its classification—whether it is positive or negative—since the theory can explain too many things, and will classify some potentially negative examples as positive. However, it *is* possible to explain a positive instance once its classification is given. Thus the theory is explanatory (Section 5.1), and the goal for learning is to determine a definition consistent with the data plus the subset of the theory that actually models the observed data. Furthermore, when there are multiple competing explanations of a given positive instance, later instances should allow determining which of the competing explanations is consistent across all data.

For example, given a can as a positive example of an object that can be placed on a table:

```
flat_bottom(canl).
small(canl).
light(canl).
```

the first step of the incremental version-space merging process uses EBG to form two rules, each corresponding to a different explanation:

```
can_put_on_table(X):-flat_bottom(X),small(X).
can_put_on_table(X):-flat_bottom(X),light(X).
```

These will be abbreviated to "[flat, small, anyweight]" and "[flat, anysize, light]". The resulting instance version space is bounded by an S-set containing these two concept definitions and a G-set containing the universal concept that says everything is an example of the concept. Intersecting this version space with the initial version space that contains all concept definitions in the concept description language simply yields the instance version space.

Returning to the first step of the learning process for the following second instance,

```
flat_bottom(cardboard_box1).
big(cardboard_box1).
light(cardboard_box1).
```

EBG can only generate one rule:

```
can_put_on_table(X):-flat_bottom(X),light(X).
```

This results in an instance version space containing [flat, anysize, light] in the *S*-set and the *G*-set containing the universal concept. Merging the two instance version spaces results in an *S*-set with the single element [flat, anysize, light] and the *G*-set containing the universal concept.

As an example of dealing with negative data with no negative-instance domain theory, consider the following negative example of can_put_on_table:

```
round_bottom(bowling_ball1).
small(bowling_ball1).
heavy(bowling_ball1).
```

The version space of concept definitions that do not include it has an *S*-set that contains the empty concept and a *G*-set that contains three concept definitions: {[flat, anysize, anyweight], [anybottom, large, anyweight], [anybottom, anysize, light]}. When merged with the version space for past data, incremental version-space merging yields a version space whose *S* set contains [flat, anysize, light] and whose *G*-set contains the two concept definitions [flat, anysize, anyweight] and [anybottom, anysize, light]. Subsequent data would further refine this version space.

5.4   Perspectives

If either empirical or analytical learning alone were sufficient for learning, there would be no reason to combine the two techniques. It is therefore useful to study and understand what each of the learning techniques offers the other beyond what they could do in isolation. From the perspective of EBG the use of incremental version-space merging addresses the imperfect theory problem (Mitchell *et al.*, 1986). From the perspective of incremental version-space merging EBG allows the use of knowledge as an explicit bias on learning.

5.4.1   Imperfect Domain Theories

The use of empirical learning in this work addresses three problems for EBG. The first is when no explanation can be found for an instance. The second is the problem of overspecialized explanations when further regularities, not explicit in the domain theory, exist for the domain. The third is when there are multiple competing explanations only one of which is correct. In all three cases this can be viewed as using empirical learning to address imperfect domain theories (Mitchell *et al.*, 1986) for EBG.

As discussed earlier, this approach can utilize examples that cannot be explained; this occurs when the domain theory can only explain a subset of the potential correctly classified instances. In such cases of incomplete domain theories the version space of concept definitions consistent with ground data, rather than their explanation-based generalizations, is formed and merged with the version space for past data. Although EBG cannot be used, the instance can still be utilized. In the extreme case when there is no domain theory the approach still applies, emulating the candidate-elimination algorithm (Chapter 3).

The second case is when explanations are overspecialized—additional regularities exist in the domain, but they are not represented in the domain theory. It, too, is a subcase of the incomplete theory problem. The assumption is that there are further regularities in the domain that empirical learning finds, perhaps covering more cases than the original theory does. Empirical learning, as done by incremental version-space merging, finds these regularities, generalizing to new situations not covered by the domain theory. New rules more general than those obtainable by EBG are formed.

The final case is a subcase of the inconsistent theory problem. It occurs with explanatory domain theories (Section 5.1) when there are multiple mutually incompatible explanations for an instance, each yielding different rules. If there are multiple competing explanations only one of which is correct, the original domain theory embodies incorrect explanations that cover situations that should not be covered. Although concept definitions consistent with each explanation are considered, the method presented here will drop those generalizations consistent with incorrect explanations if they are not consistent with later data.

5.4.2 Biasing Search

The alternative way to view this approach to combining empirical and analytical learning is from the perspective of empirical learning, asking what contributions analytical learning makes to empirical learning. The answer is that analytical learning hastens convergence to a final concept definition. Rather than updating the version space—doing empirical learning—with single instances, each instance has the effect of multiple instances. It can be shown that updating a version space with the explanation-based generalization of an instance yields the same new version space as updating the version space with all (ungeneralized) instances that have the same explanation as the original instance. In this view the power of the analytical learning method is to allow convergence to a final concept definition using fewer instances.

This becomes clear from the perspective of *bias* (Mitchell, 1980; Utgoff, 1986). Bias is a label for whatever allows a learning system to generalize beyond the data. For example, restricting concept definitions to pure conjunctions does not permit expressing disjunctive definitions, effectively ruling out such potential candidate definitions. Given two instances, the learning system cannot simply form a disjunction of the instances, but must rather find a conjunctive description that covers both instances. In most cases this requires including new unseen instances in the generalization.

The effect of bias on version space methods is in the space of generalizations; the stronger the bias, the fewer candidate generalizations that are considered. As described above, the combination of analytical and empirical learning discussed here behaves like the pure candidate-elimination algorithm given no knowledge, but when knowledge is provided and applicable, the version spaces considered are smaller. Concept definitions are removed from consideration due to the knowledge. For example, concept definitions that only cover a single instance will no longer be considered—only those concept definitions reflecting all instances covered by the explanation-based generalization of the instance are considered. The more specific portions of version spaces are excluded for positive instances, and the more general portions are excluded for negative instances. After each instance more of the version space of candidate concept definitions is ruled out, requiring fewer instances to converge to a final concept definition. Thus the knowledge used by EBG provides an additional bias beyond that imposed by the concept description language.

From a slightly different perspective, bias can simply be viewed as whatever one can point to as justification for the results of learning. For example, the bias for the candidate-elimination algorithm is its concept description language—if one believes that the desired concept is express-ible in the language, then one must believe the result of learning (assum-ing the data is consistent). For EBG, the bias is the knowledge given to the system—if one believes that the knowledge is correct, then one must believe the result of learning. In the work described here the two biases are combined—if one believes the knowledge (or at least the subset of the knowledge that models the data in the case of explanatory theories) and that the desired concept is expressible in the given language, then one must believe the result of learning. Knowledge provides an explicit bias for em-pirical learning on top of that of the concept description language.

This view of knowledge as bias suggests a method for measuring the strength the of domain theories used in the manner described in this chapter. Recent theoretical work on concept learning (e.g., (Haussler, 1986)) has developed quantitative theories of bias. For example, the Vapnik-Cher-vonenkis dimension provides one way to measure the bias implicit in a learning system. The idea here would be to use such a quantitative theory of bias to measure explicitly the bias of a learning system both with and without knowledge. The difference gives the additional bias provided by the knowledge. This is an area for future work.

5.5 Constraints on the Concept Description Language

As mentioned in Section 5.2, there are constraints on the form elements of the concept description language may take. These constraints arise from two sources: constraints on the form the results of EBG may take, and constraints due to computational tractability.

Like much work in concept learning (especially with version spaces), this chapter has assumed that the concept description language is conjunctive. This is due to both the usual computational reasons (computing minimal generalizations, maximal specializations, and relative generality in such languages is often inexpensive), as well as the fact that EBG generates implications whose antecedents are conjunctions. This work makes an assumption similar to the single-representation trick (Dietterich *et al.*, 1982): that all possible results of EBG are in the concept description language. Without such an assumption it would be necessary to find the most specific terms in the language consistent with results of EBG. In theory the approach described here would work with any language, but determining version spaces may be difficult.

However, the restriction on concept description language in this work is even stronger than simply requiring conjunctions. Arbitrary conjunctions can be NP-complete just to test for relative generality (for example, comparing arbitrary conjunctions of On(x, y), where the same variable may appear in multiple conjuncts). Therefore this work further restricts the language (by restricting the form domain theories for EBG may take) to conjunctions of unary predicates over a fixed set of features, where each feature can appear at most once. Again, in theory any language would work, but for practical considerations such restrictions are necessary.

5.6   Related Work

Most similar to this work is Mitchell's (1984) proposal for combining empirical and analytical learning of search control. Mitchell proposed applying analytical learning to raw data, then doing incremental empirical learning on the generalized data. In addition to simply implementing Mitchell's proposal, the technique presented here goes beyond Mitchell's original proposal, handling incomplete theories as well as inconsistent theories when there are multiple conflicting explanations for a single instance.

Also similar to this work is Anderson's (Anderson, 1983; Anderson, 1986) generalization technique for tuning productions in ACT*. Whenever ACT*'s knowledge compilation mechanisms form a new production, the production is compared to productions already in memory to check if any are similar. If a similar production is found, ACT* generalizes the two productions to form a new, more general result. ACT* is fairly liberal in generating new, more general (potentially overgeneral) productions for two reasons. First, new productions are added to memory with very low strength; the new production must prove itself by being useful in future cases, in which case its strength is increased. Second, ACT* has a discrimination mechanism for tuning productions; additional conditions are added to overgeneral productions that conflict with other productions.

Cohen's (1990) work on using EBG as an abstraction mechanism provides an approach to combining empirical and analytical learning that is similar to this work, but avoids as strong restrictions on the concept description language. His approach applies EBG to all positive data and generalizes each result further (in multiple ways) by operations on the example's proof tree (such as dropping selected subproofs so that their weakest preconditions do not appear in the final result). Cohen's system then selects a subset of all such generalized results that correctly classify the training data, using a greedy set-cover algorithm. Since his technique never attempts to compare two concept definitions or find the minimal generalization or maximal specialization of two descriptions, it does not require the concept description language restrictions necessary here.

The IOE method of Flann and Dietterich (1990) also bears some resemblance to this work. In contrast, however, IOE generalizes across *explanations*, rather than across the results of EBG on those explanations. If a constant appears in all explanations, it will remain in IOE's generalization, even if EBG would have variablized the constant. IOE forms rules that are never more general that what EBG can create. In their view explanations are overgeneral, and IOE will find specializations of such explanations. This work instead finds concept definitions more general than the results of EBG. However, extensions to their work could permit generalizing beyond what appears in the explanation, to obtain results similar to those given here.

The use of domain theories in this work is similar to the use of half-order theories in MetaDENDRAL (Buchanan and Mitchell, 1978). The task for MetaDENDRAL is to form rules that accurately predict how molecules fragment in a mass spectrometer. MetaDENDRAL begins with an overgeneral half-order theory—an explanatory theory (Section 5.1)—that says almost every bond in a molecule will break. MetaDENDRAL, using its INTSUM procedure, forms fairly specific rules for each peak in a mass spectrum for a molecule, and then generalizes (using RULEGEN and RULEMOD) the rules to form a specialization of the half-order theory that best models the data. The similarities to this work are two-fold. The first is its use of the half-order theory to process the data to form specific rules for each peak—comparable to the use of EBG on data in this work. The second similarity is in the high-level task of forming specializations of an overgeneral explanatory theory to model data.

As pointed out earlier, this work can be viewed as using domain theories as an explicit form of bias on empirical learning, and is thus reminiscent of the use of determinations by Russell and Grosof (1987) to bias empirical learning. However, rather than forming the biased generalization space at the start as they propose, this work imposes the bias on each instance by converting it into a form consistent with the bias. The comparable method using determinations would be to form single-instance generalizations (Russell, 1987) of each instance using determinations, then doing empirical learning on the generalized instance as is done here.

Others have explored combining empirical and analytical learning to solve additional problems they have when used in isolation. For example, OCCAM (Pazzani, 1988) uses empirical learning when no analytical learning can be done. UNIMEM (Lebowitz, 1986) on the other hand uses empirical learning to focus the search for an explanation for analytical learning. Both these systems use empirical learning to address shortcomings of analytical learning. In contrast, Danyluk (1987) uses the results of analytical learning to suggest preferences among the predicates considered by empirical learning, and thus uses analytical learning to aid empirical learning.

5.7   Summary

This chapter has described one approach to combining empirical and analytical learning, using incremental version-space merging. The central idea is to apply EBG to training data, then do empirical learning on the generalized data. This process permits the use of incomplete and inconsistent domain theories in analytical learning, and utilizes empirical learning to handle such domain-theory imperfections. The combination can also be viewed as allowing the use of knowledge as an explicit bias in learning. The combination approach is capable of exhibiting behavior along a spectrum from knowledge-free to knowledge-rich learning, depending on the amount of knowledge given to the learner.

Chapter 6

Incremental Batch Learning

Chapters 3 through 5 have described how incremental version-space merging can be used to learn incrementally from a sequence of training instances. More generally, however, the information processed by incremental version-space merging need not correspond directly training data; as long as a piece of information can be converted into a version space of viable concept definitions it can be used by incremental version-space merging.

This chapter describes the use of a second learning method as a source of information about a target concept. In contrast to the previous chapters, here individual version spaces are generated by running this second learning method on *sets* of data. Each run provides information about the target concept, and these different pieces of information are integrated using incremental version-space merging. This use of incremental version-space merging might best be called "incremental batch learning" (Clearwater *et al.*, 1989), in that rather than learning from individual instances, incremental version-space merging intersects version spaces corresponding to batches of instances. RL (Fu, 1985) is the learning method used to form individual version spaces in the experiments of this chapter.

6.1   RL

Anomalous data can occur for many reasons. Even as simple a reason as poor typing can yield inconsistent data. Chapter 4 described an approach for learning from data with bounded inconsistency. It does not permit discounting or removing anomalous data. In cases of *unbounded* inconsistency some of the data are erroneous and must be ignored. Learning methods that handle such inconsistent data form concept definitions that perform well, although not perfectly, on the data, viewing those instances not covered correctly as anomalous.

RL (Fu, 1985) is an example of such a learning method. Based on the approach taken by MetaDENDRAL (Buchanan and Mitchell, 1978), RL starts with the most general concept definition that covers all instances, and explores its specializations to find those that cover some minimum percentage of positive instances and some maximum percentage of negative instances. Given these user-supplied thresholds on the desired accuracy of the rules to be learned—some limit on the maximum number of negative instances that may be covered and the least number of positive instances that must be covered—RL returns the set of most general or most specific (depending on the user's desire) concept definitions satisfying the thresholds. These two sets of concept definitions bound (i.e., form the boundary sets for) the version space of concept definitions satisfying the given thresholds.

6.2   The Approach

The central idea here is to use RL to form version spaces for different sets of data, then combine the results using incremental version-space merging. This is done by running RL twice for each of the sets, one time asking for the set of most specific concept definitions that satisfy the particular thresholds (maximum false positive and false negative rates) set for learning, and the second time requesting the set of most general concept definitions that satisfy the thresholds. This generates a version space for each set of data, containing all concept definitions that satisfy the given thresholds. After doing this on each set, incremental version-space merging is used to intersect the resulting version spaces, yielding the most specific and most general concept definitions that satisfy the thresholds across each set of data. This final version space is returned as the result of learning.

The approach can be stated as follows:

1. Use RL to form the version space of all concept definitions satisfying the thresholds on the given set of data.

2. Intersect this version space with the version space generated for past runs of RL on other sets of data.

3. Return to the first step for the next set of the data.

6.3   Example

The particular domain used for testing this combination of RL and incremental version-space merging is the formation of rules for the diagnosis of accelerator beam lines, originally investigated using RL alone (Buchanan *et al.*, 1988). The task is to find rules that can locate errors in the particle beam lines used in high-energy physics given examples of beam lines with and without errors.

6.3.1   Domain

Instances are described by four real-valued attributes, one in the range 0 to 10, and three in the range 0 to 100. They describe various features of a beam-line during a run. The concept description language is the same as was used by Buchanan *et al.*, and divides the attribute values into discrete ranges of the form $a < x \leq b$, where for each of the features a and b can only take on one of seven prespecified values (called *markers*), including the endpoints of the range of legal values the feature may take. For example, the first feature, with range 0 to 10, has the seven markers 0.0, 0.3, 0.5, 0.7, 1.0, 2.0, and 10.0. There is a further restriction that a and b must be "adjacent" markers to be legal, that is, that no other marker exists between the markers used in a particular range, or instead one of a or b must be an endpoint marker. This is equivalent to saying that if a and b are not adjacent, the feature must either be of the form $a < x$ or $x \leq b$. Thus for the feature mentioned above both $0.0 < x \leq 0.7$ and $0.3 < x \leq 0.5$ are legal, whereas $0.3 < x \leq 0.7$ is not. The concept description language contains all concept definitions that are conjunctions of legal ranges over at most three of the four attributes. Four 150-instance training sets were generated by a FORTRAN simulation of a beam line. Approximately 20% are positive examples of a particular error type (an "element error") and 80% are negative examples that do not have that error present.

6.3.2 Method

RL was run on each of the four data sets, generating the most general and most specific concept definitions that satisfied the thresholds. The particular thresholds used on learning were that no rule should cover less than 80% of the positive examples, and that no rule should cover more than 10% of the negative examples. The resulting four version spaces were then intersected using incremental version-space merging, yielding a single version space of all concept definitions that satisfied the thresholds for all four sets of data.

6.3.3 Results

Since RL has already been used on this task, the obvious standard for comparison was to see how well the results after incremental version-space merging compare to those of RL alone on the combined set of instances. Thus, in addition to the RL runs on the smaller sets, RL was run using the same thresholds on the union of the sets of data, yielding the version space of all concept definitions that satisfy the thresholds across the combined data set.

Both RL alone and RL with incremental version-space merging generate version spaces. A version space is just a set of concept definitions; some rule or rules must be selected out of the version space as the result of learning. The selection technique used by Buchanan *et al.*, and thus the technique used here, was to take the set of most general concept definitions as a disjunctive definition for the concept. If any is true for an instance, then a prediction is made that the concept (a particular type of error in the beam line) is true. The predictive accuracy of these disjunctions were compared on a test set of 586 preclassified instances. The testing was done twice, first for the results of pure RL, and then a second time for the results of incremental version-space merging.

The overall prediction rate was 81.9% for the results of incremental version-space merging, whereas the results of RL alone yielded a 79.4% prediction rate. Both generated 99.0% accuracy on positive alone, but the incremental version-space merging results incorrectly covered 21.6% of the negatives to pure RL's 25.7%. This large false positive rate is to be expected, since the final rule is a disjunction of already very general rules (where the reasoning for using general rules is that false positives are less costly than false negatives.) Thus the two approaches generated similar results. These results are summarized in Table 6.1

Learner	Pos %	Neg %	Overall %
IVSM	99.0	21.6	81.9
RL	99.0	25.7	79.4

Table 6.1. Beam-Line Results.

6.3.4 Analysis

The version space resulting from the combined RL/incremental version-space merging approach will always be a subset of the one obtained by pure RL if the same thresholds are used. The method for selecting rules from the version space is known to generate overly general rules for the beam-line learning task. Buchanan *et al.* (1988) use a second technique that conjoins different overly general concept definitions to form more specific rules. This work can be viewed as an alternative way to specialize the results of RL in this task. Since the incremental version-space merging version space is a subset of the RL version space, the disjunction of the G-set elements for the former will always be a specialization of the disjunction generated from the latter.

6.4 Summary

This chapter has shown how incremental version-space merging can be used to combine the results of a second learning method used on different sets of data. The insight is to view the second learning method as specifying sets of viable concept definitions that are encoded as version spaces and given to incremental version-space merging. This demonstrates the use of incremental version-space merging on sources of information that do not correspond directly to individual training instances.

Chapter 7

Computational Complexity

This chapter analyzes the computational complexity of incremental version-space merging. Incremental version-space merging has two major steps: version-space formation, and version-space intersection. The computational complexity of each of these is first discussed, followed by an analysis of the complexity of the overall incremental version-space merging method.

7.1 Version-Space Formation

The first step of each iteration of incremental version-space merging is to form the version space of concept definitions to consider given the current piece of information. Since this occurs at each step, it is clearly necessary for it to be feasible computationally. A general analysis of the complexity of this step is impossible—it depends both on the specific method for generating version spaces and on the particular concept description language being used. However, it is possible to do this analysis for specific approaches, and that is what will be done here.

The version-space-formation method to be considered here is the one used in the learning tasks of Chapters 3, 4, and 5. The particular method works for conjunctive languages over a fixed set of k features, and handles the case when each version space is effectively the union of n version spaces (as occurred with ambiguous data, data with bounded inconsistency, and EBG with multiple explanations).

For positive instances the algorithm initially takes as the S-set the union of the most specific terms in the concept description that may be considered for the instance. In the case of ambiguous data using the single-representation trick (Dietterich *et al.*, 1982) this is the set of potential identities the instance might be; for bounded inconsistency this is the set of most specific terms consistent with the instance or one of its neighbors; for EBG this is the set of results of EBG across all explanations for the instance. If there are n possibilities, the maximum size of S will be n. However, in some cases it is necessary to check if any element of the S-set is more general than another element (such as when dealing with multiple explanations for EBG). The number of comparisons of relative generality made by the algorithm for doing this is proportional to the square of the number of elements in the S-set, and thus at most n^2 comparisons of relative generality will be made.

To complete this analysis it is necessary to determine the time it takes to compute a single test of relative generality. If there are k conjuncts for elements of the concept description language, then k feature comparisons must be made. In the case where features are ranges of the form $a \le x < b$ (such as in Chapter 4), such comparisons take constant time, and thus computing the S-set takes time proportional to at most $n^2 k$. In contrast, in the case of tree-structured features (such as in Chapters 3 and 5), each feature comparison takes time proportional to the height h of the tree-structured hierarchy for that feature. However, h is at most $\log v$, where v is the maximum number of values any feature can take on.[1] Therefore the time to compare two concept descriptions takes time proportional to at most $k \log v$. Thus computing an S-set for tree-structured features takes at most time proportional to $n^2 k \log v$. As long as forming the set of possible identities is tractable, handling positive data is tractable.

For negative instances the algorithm is more complicated. When only a single identity must be considered for an instance (e.g., when there is no ambiguity) the algorithm explores all ways to specialize each attribute of the universal concept to exclude the instance. For example, in the robot grasping domain of Chapter 3 there are three ways to specialize the shape

---

[1]Of course, this is only a useful bound on h when v is finite.

attribute to exclude octahedron: sphere, cube, and pyramid. If there are on average b possible ways to specialize a feature to exclude a value, and there are k features, then there will be at most kb ways to specialize the universal concept to exclude the given instance, and thus kb elements in the new G-set.[2] When the individual version space must effectively be the union of n version spaces, the resulting G-set will have at most nkb elements.

However, the G-set should only have maximal elements: one specialization of the universal concept (e.g., based on one possible identity of an ambiguous instance) may be more specific than another. Such nonmaximal concept definitions must be pruned. The number of comparisons made by the algorithm used to remove nonmaximal elements is proportional to the square of the size of G-set. In the case where features are ranges of the form $a \leq x < b$, with the range of x discretized to a fixed set of values (such as measuring values to the nearest millimeter in Chapter 4), $b \leq 2$ and comparing two concept descriptions takes time proportional to k. Therefore the time to compute a G-set is proportional to at most $n^2 k^3$. In the case of tree-structured features (Chapters 3 and 5), b is at most $(w - 1) \log v$, where w is the maximum branching factor for all feature hierarchies, and comparing two concept descriptions of at most k conjuncts takes time proportional to at most $k \log v$; therefore computing the G-set requires time proportional to $(nk(w - 1) \log v)^2 k \log v = (n(w - 1))^2 (k \log v)^3$. In both cases, this is feasible as long as determining the n possibilities is tractable.

7.2   Version-Space Merging

The second step of incremental version-space merging is to intersect two version spaces using the version-space merging algorithm. The complexity of version-space merging is again dependent on the particular concept description language. The algorithm computes for the new S-set the most specific common generalization of pairs from the two S-sets that are covered by some element of each of the G-sets but not by some other element of the new S-set, and does a symmetrical process for the G-sets.

---

[2]If b is infinite (e.g., when the number of values v a feature may take is infinite), the use of version spaces inappropriate, since boundary-set sizes must be finite.

For both tree-structured features and features of the form $a \leq x < b$ the minimal common generalization of two concept descriptions is unique. Therefore, if there are m_1 and m_2 elements in the two initial S-sets, there are at most $m_1 m_2$ in the resulting unpruned S-set. The overall time to compute the pruned S-set is the sum of the time to compute the elements of the unpruned S-set plus the time to compute its minimal elements plus the time to prune those that are not more specific that some element of the two G-sets. Computing the minimal elements of the S-set requires at most $(m_1 m_2)^2$ comparisons. The resulting partially pruned S-set will contain at most $m_1 m_2$ elements after this process, and if there are n_1 and n_2 elements in the two initial G-sets, the process that removes uncovered S-set elements makes an additional $m_1 m_2 (n_1 + n_2)$ comparisons. Thus at most $(m_1 m_2)^2 + m_1 m_2 (n_1 + n_2)$ comparisons must be made.

When features are of the form $a \leq x < b$, comparisons take time proportional to the number of features k, as does the process that computes the minimal generalization of two concept definitions. Computing the resulting S-set therefore takes time proportional to at most $m_1 m_2 k + (m_1 m_2)^2 k + m_1 m_2 (n_1 + n_2) k$. Since the process is symmetric for the G-set, its complexity is proportional to at most $n_1 n_2 k + (n_1 n_2)^2 k + n_1 n_2 (m_1 + m_2) k$. Whichever is greater is the overriding term for the complexity of the merging process for languages consisting of conjunctions of features of the form $a \leq x < b$.

When features are tree-structured, comparisons take time proportional to $k \log v$, where v is the maximum number of values any feature may take. The process that computes the minimal generalization of two concept definitions takes time proportional to $k \log^2 k$. Computing the resulting S-set therefore takes time proportional to $m_1 m_2 k \log^2 v + (m_1 m_2)^2 k \log v + m_1 m_2 (n_1 + n_2) k \log v$. The G-set case is nearly symmetric, with the exception that computing the maximal specialization of two concept definitions takes time proportional to at most $k \log v$, so the overall complexity is proportional to at most $n_1 n_2 k \log v + (n_1 n_2)^2 k \log v + n_1 n_2 (m_1 + m_2) k \log v$. Whichever is greater is the overriding term for the complexity of the merging process for languages consisting of conjunctions of tree-structure features.

7.3   Incremental Version-Space Merging

The preceding two sections discussed the complexity of the individual steps taken during each iteration of incremental version-space merging. The complexity of the overall algorithm given a set of instances is a more difficult issue. It depends on the nature of the concept being learned, the concept description language, and the particular instances provided as data. In the worst case the process will be exponential in the number of instances, as has been pointed out by Haussler (1988) for the candidate-elimination algorithm, which is subsumed by this work.

7.3.1   Exponential Boundary-Set Growth

Haussler presents a simple learning scenario—a concept description language and instance sequence—where the size of the G boundary set for the original version-space approach grows exponentially with the number of instances. Since the approach described here subsumes the original version-space approach, it, too, can face such problems.

Haussler's scenario uses a concept description language with $2n$ Boolean features $A_1, \ldots, A_{2n}$. There are $n + 1$ instances, one positive and n negative. The single positive instance, presented first, has all attributes true. For each of the negative instances, the ith instance has the $2i-1^{st}$ and $2i^{th}$ attributes false and the rest true. After each instance is processed the G-set doubles in size, and the final G-set after processing all $n + 1$ instances has 2^n concept definitions. For each concept definition either the $2i-1^{st}$ attribute or the $2i^{th}$ attribute is true and the other is a "don't care," which will match both true and false attribute values. The G-set contains all such concept definitions.

There are two question that can be asked. The first is how often this situation arises for a particular learning task and instance sequence. This can only be asked in the context of the learning task and instance sequence. The second question is whether, even when such a worst-case situation arises, it can be avoided.

One possible approach to this second problem is to note that in some cases where exponential growth could occur, it is possible to order the data so that exponential growth is avoided. If such an ordering scheme takes time polynomial in the number of instances, the difficulty has been avoided. One example where this is true (for consistent data) is in cases where after processing all the given data the resulting boundary sets are singleton. In such cases the data can always be ordered (in polynomial time) to guarantee that the boundary sets will remain singleton. (The ordering algorithm basically processes positive data first, then processes negative "near-misses" (Winston, 1975) that remove selected "don't cares.") This is even true if Haussler's data set is a subset of the full data set.

This is an area of current work. The knowledge that the final boundary sets are singleton is strong. Weaker information that results in similar polynomial-time guarantees is desirable.

In addition to Haussler's exponentially growing boundary-set scenario above, he also presents a theorem that appears to be a serious negative result for version spaces. The simple statement of the theorem is that finding any minimal-length conjunctive concept definition consistent with a set of data is NP-hard. Since for conjunctive languages G-sets contain all such minimal-length conjunctions consistent with data, the result seems to make the use of version spaces futile, since determining even one element of the G-set is NP-hard.

The general idea of Haussler's proof is to show that any minimal set cover problem (known to be NP-complete) can be solved if a solution to the minimal-length conjunction problem exists. The key observation that lessens the generality of Haussler's result is that the set cover problem is mapped to a *subset* of the minimal-conjunction problem. That subset is NP-hard, but other subsets need not be. The specific subset that Haussler uses is when the set of data contains one positive and k negative instances. It is only this subset of minimal-conjunction problems that Haussler has shown to be NP-hard. Note further that even this NP-hard subset of minimal-conjunction problems can still contain cases that are solvable in polynomial time.

7.3.2 Intractable Domains

Even when boundary sets do not grow exponentially in size there are techniques for further improving the performance of incremental version-space merging. Two have been explored: skipping data that do not change the version space, and selecting data that decrease boundary set size. In the iris learning example of Chapter 4 such intelligent instance selection cut the time for learning from hours to only a few minutes.

The first step taken to process the iris data was to remove redundant data. As an example of this, when two instances yield the same version space only one need be considered. A degenerate case of this is when two instances are identical. More generally, whenever one instance version space is a superset of another the first instance can be removed. It will never yield any additional information beyond that provided by the second instance. The simple way to view this is that, since incremental version-space merging is just set intersection, intersecting set A with both a second set B and a subset C of B yields the same result as ignoring B and only intersecting A and C.

This step was a significant time-saver, at times eliminating up to 80% of the data. Note that the test for superset/subset is simple to do in boundary-set representation: version space VS_1 is a superset of VS_2 if, for each element of VS_1's S-set, there is some element of VS_2's S-set more general than it, and similarly all elements of VS_1's G-set have some element of VS_2's G-set more specific than it.

Related to this is the observation that as learning proceeds and the version space decreases in size, some instances will have no affect on learning. Those instances that are classified the same by all members of the version space will not change the version space (assuming that the version space will not collapse to the empty set), and therefore can be skipped. Since incremental version-space merging just does set intersection, if an instance will not affect the version space, its version space must be a superset of the current version space. Thus, before the potentially expensive use of version-space merging, the implementation of incremental version-space merging used in this work first checks that the current instance version space is not a superset of the current version space. If it is, the instance is ignored. This, too, results in a significant reduction in the number of instances that need be processed.

The second time-saving technique explored in this work is based on the observation that, since the complexity of version-space merging is a function of boundary-set size, obtaining small boundary sets is a good idea. Furthermore, practice shows that once the boundary sets reach small size they typically stay small. Two specific heuristics were used that were generally successful in this task: selecting instances with small boundary sets, and selecting instances that have boundary sets with some overlap with the current version-space boundary sets.

The reason for the first heuristic is simple: since the complexity is a product of the sizes of the boundary sets, smaller ones are better. The second heuristic is based on the fact that when two boundary sets overlap, the pairwise minimal generalizations (if the overlap is in the S-set) for pairs *not* involved in the overlap were typically subsumed by the given overlap, since the minimal common generalization of an element in the overlap with itself just returns the overlapped item, with no further generalization required. The general topic of instance selection and ordering is an area of continuing research. Note, however, that the general problem of ordering training data to yield optimal learning is NP-hard.

7.4 Summary

This chapter has addressed the computational complexity of incremental version-space merging. In addition to an analysis of the worst-case complexity of the technique, it also discussed Haussler's (1988) negative results for version spaces and showed why they are not as serious as they might at first seem. The chapter concluded with a discussion of heuristic techniques for improving the performance of the approach.

Chapter 8

Theoretical Underpinnings

This chapter presents the theoretical underpinnings of the generalized version-space approach. It begins with the necessary and sufficient conditions under which an arbitrary set of concept definitions from a concept description language can be represented by boundary sets. This forms the new definition of version spaces. The chapter continues with an analysis of the conditions under which the intersection of two version spaces is a version space, presents a formal description of the version-space merging algorithm (Section 2.2), the method for computing the intersection in boundary-set representation, and proves that it is correct. Similar results are given for version-space unions, which forms the basis for dealing with ambiguous information.

8.1 Terminology and Notation

Throughout this chapter CDL is used to refer to the (potentially infinite) set of concept definitions describable in the concept description language and considered in the concept learning task. There is a space of possible objects (instances), and each concept definition divides a set of objects into those objects it covers and those it does not. The subset of the entire space of possible objects that a concept definition covers is known as its *extension*. Concept definitions are partially ordered by generality, written "$\preceq$." "$C_1 \preceq C_2$" should be read as "C_1 is less general than or equal to C_2," which means

83

that the extension of C_1 is a subset of the extension of C_2. "$C_1 \prec C_2$," "$C_1 \succeq C_2$," and "$C_1 \succ C_2$" have similar, obvious meanings.

> **Theorem 8.1 (Mitchell, 1978):** *The relation $\preceq$ is a partial ordering.*

Proof: The reflexivity, asymmetry, and transitivity fall out of the definition of $\preceq$ using subset. Since the subset relation is a partial order, so, too, is $\preceq$ a partial order. $\square$

The concept learning problem is to identify one concept definition out of the set of potential concept definitions in the *CDL*, given information from some outside source about the nature of the unknown concept. Usually this information is of the form of positive and negative examples of this target concept, that is, classified training data of the concept.

8.2   Generalizing Version Spaces

This section presents criteria that, if satisfied by a subset of a concept description language, define that subset to be a version space, and hence representable by boundary sets. First, however, it is necessary to define two terms, closed and bounded. A version space will be defined as any subset of a concept description language that is closed and bounded. This then will be shown to imply that the set can be represented by boundary sets.

8.2.1   Closure

A set C of concept definitions in the *CDL* is said to be *closed* if, given any two elements of C, any element of the concept description language between them (in the partial order) is also in C. This basically says that there are no "holes" in the set. More formally:

> **Definition 8.1:** *A subset $C \subseteq CDL$ is said to be closed if and only if for all $c_1, c_2 \in C$, $c_3 \in CDL$, $c_1 \preceq c_3 \preceq c_2$ implies $c_3 \in C$.*

Examples:

1. If the *CDL* is the set of all closed ranges over a single real-valued attribute x of the form "$\{x \mid a \leq x \leq b\}$" where a and b are reals:

   (a) If $C = CDL$, then C is closed.

   (b) If $C = \{c \in CDL \mid a, b \text{ are integers}\}$, then C is not closed, since between any two concept definitions there will be another whose range delimiters a and b are reals.

   (c) If $C = \{c \in CDL \mid a \geq 0, b \leq 1000\}$, then C is closed.

2. Given any *CDL*, if C is the set of all concept definitions consistent with a set of classified instances (i.e., Mitchell's original notion of version space), C is closed.

8.2.2 Boundedness

To define boundedness, it is necessary to state what the minimal and maximal elements of a partially ordered set are:

Definition 8.2: *The set of minimal elements of C is written* $\text{Min}(C)$, *and is defined by*

$$\text{Min}(C) = \{c \in C \mid \neg \exists c' \in C \text{ such that } c' \prec c\}.$$

Similarly, the set of maximal elements of C, $\text{Max}(C)$, is

$$\text{Max}(C) = \{c \in C \mid \neg \exists c' \in C \text{ such that } c' \succ c\}.$$

C is said to be *bounded* by $S = \text{Min}(C)$ and $G = \text{Max}(C)$ if all elements of C are greater than or equal to some element of S and less than or equal to some element of G. More formally:

Definition 8.3: *C is bounded (by $S = \text{Min}(C)$ and $G = \text{Max}(C)$) if and only if for all $c \in C$ there exists some $s \in S$ and some $g \in G$ such that $s \preceq c \preceq g$.*

Examples:

1. If the *CDL* is the set of closed ranges of the form $\{x \mid a \leq x \leq b\}$ where a and b are reals:

   (a) If $C = CDL$, then C is not bounded, since $G = \{\}$ (for every concept definition in the language there is another concept definition more general than it), and thus for every element $c \in C$ there is no $g \in G$ with $c \preceq g$.

   (b) If $C = \{c \in CDL \mid a, b \text{ are integers}\}$, then $G = \{\}$, so C is not bounded.

   (c) If $C = \{c \in CDL \mid a \geq 0, b \leq 1000\}$, then $S = \{\{0\}, \ldots, \{1000\}\}$, $G = \{\{x \mid 0 \leq x \leq 1000\}\}$, and C is bounded (by S and G).

2. If the *CDL* is the set of all conjunctive expressions over a finite set of boolean features, then all subsets $C \subseteq CDL$ are bounded.

This second example is a simple result of the following theorem:

Theorem 8.2: *If the CDL is finite (i.e., there are only a finite number of concept definitions expressible) then all subsets C of the CDL are bounded.*

Proof: By induction on the size of C. $\square$

The concept of bounded is closely related to Mitchell's (1978) notion of *admissibility*. Specifically, Mitchell defines admissibility to be a property of concept description languages—whether *all* subsets of the language can be represented by boundary sets. The concept of bounded applies to *subsets* of the concept description language. It is possible to have languages with subsets that are not bounded, yet also with some subsets that *are* bounded. The important thing to guarantee is that only bounded subsets will be used during the particular learning task at hand. Admissibility is a stronger restriction.

8.2.3 Version Spaces

It is now possible to present the new definition for version spaces:

> **Definition 8.4:** *A subset C of a CDL is a version space if and only if C is closed and bounded.*

Note that this definition subsumes Mitchell's definition of version space—any set of concept definitions in an admissible language consistent with data is closed and bounded.

The benefit of the original form of version spaces was that any version space could be represented by only retaining its minimal and maximal elements—the boundary sets. This remains true for this new form of version spaces. To show this it is necessary to state precisely what it means to be representable by boundary sets:

> **Definition 8.5:** *A set $C \subseteq CDL$ is said to be representable by boundary sets S and G if and only if*
>
> $$C = \{c \in CDL \mid \exists s \in S, g \in G \text{ such that } s \preceq c \preceq g\}.$$

This definition states that C is representable by boundary sets if the set of elements between the minimal and maximal elements of C gives back C.

It can now be shown that any version space—i.e., any closed, bounded subset $C \subseteq CDL$—can be represented by boundary sets:

> **Theorem 8.3:** *All closed, bounded subsets C of a CDL can be represented by boundary sets.*

Proof: Showing that a set C can be represented by boundary sets $S = \text{Min}(C)$ and $G = \text{Max}(C)$, is done by first demonstrating that

$$C \subseteq \{c \in CDL \mid \exists s \in S, g \in G \text{ such that } s \preceq c \preceq g\},$$

then demonstrating that

$$C \supseteq \{c \in CDL \mid \exists s \in S, g \in G \text{ such that } s \preceq c \preceq g\}.$$

First the $\subseteq$: If $c' \in C$ then there exists an s in S and g in G such that $s \preceq c' \preceq g$ (since C is bounded). Furthermore, since $c' \in C$ and $C \subseteq CDL$, $c' \in CDL$. Therefore

$$c' \in \{c \in CDL \mid \exists s \in S, g \in G \text{ such that } s \preceq c \preceq g\},$$

so

$$C \subseteq \{c \in CDL \mid \exists s \in S, g \in G \text{ such that } s \preceq c \preceq g\}.$$

For the $\supseteq$:

$$c' \in \{c \in CDL \mid \exists s \in S, g \in G \text{ such that } s \preceq c \preceq g\}$$

means that there is an s in S for which $s \preceq c'$ and a g in G where $c' \preceq g$. Since $S, G \subseteq C$, $s, g \in C$. Since C is closed, this means that $c' \in C$, and thus that

$$C \supseteq \{c \in CDL \mid \exists s \in S, g \in G \text{ such that } s \preceq c \preceq g\}.$$

$\square$

The converse can also be shown to be true, namely, that all subsets $C \subseteq CDL$ that can be represented by boundary sets are closed and bounded. This demonstrates that closure and boundedness are both necessary and sufficient conditions on when an arbitrary subset of a *CDL* can be represented by boundary sets.

Theorem 8.4: *All subsets C of a CDL that can be represented by boundary sets are closed and bounded.*

Proof: The boundedness portion of the proof is trivial. For all $c \in C$ there exists $s \in S = \text{Min}(C)$ and $g \in G = \text{Max}(C)$ such that $s \preceq c \preceq g$ (since C can be represented by boundary sets). This is for any $c \in C$. Thus C is bounded by S and G. For closure: Given $c_1, c_2 \in C$, it is necessary to show for all $c_3 \in CDL$ when $c_1 \preceq c_3 \preceq c_2$, $c_3 \in C$. Since $c_1 \in C$ and C can be represented by boundary sets, there exists $s \in S$ such that $s \preceq c_1$. Similarly there exists $g \in G$ such that $c_2 \preceq g$. Since $c_1 \preceq c_3 \preceq c_2$, $s \preceq c_3 \preceq g$. But by the definition of "representable by boundary sets" this means $c_3 \in C$. $\square$

8.3 Version-Space Intersections

This section presents conditions under which the intersection of two version spaces is a version space, and provides a method for doing this intersection in boundary-set representation. It is first useful to note that the intersection of two version spaces is always closed:

> **Theorem 8.5:** *Given two version spaces VS_1 and VS_2, their intersection $VS_1 \cap VS_2$ is closed.*

Proof: $VS_1 \cap VS_2$ is closed if for all $c_1 \in VS_1 \cap VS_2$, $c_2 \in VS_1 \cap VS_2$, and $c_3 \in CDL$, $c_1 \preceq c_3 \preceq c_2$ implies $c_3 \in VS_1 \cap VS_2$. Since both c_1 and c_2 are in $VS_1 \cap VS_2$, they are both in VS_1 and VS_2. Since both VS_1 and VS_2 are closed (since they are version spaces), $c_3 \in VS_1$ and $c_3 \in VS_2$. But this means $c_3 \in VS_1 \cap VS_2$. □

A simple corollary of this is

> **Corollary 8.1:** *The intersection of two version spaces is a version space if and only if the intersection is bounded.*

Note that the intersection of two version spaces VS_1 and VS_2 is not necessarily bounded. To see this consider the concept description language in which concept definitions are closed ranges of reals over a single variable x of the form "$\{x \mid a \leq x \leq b\}$" (i.e., "$\{x \mid x \in [a, b]\}$") if the size of the range is less than or equal to some n, and open ranges of reals over the variable x of the form "$\{x \mid a < x < b\}$" (i.e., "$\{x \mid x \in (a, b)\}$") if the size of the range is greater than n. For example, if $n = 5$, and VS_1 contains all concept definitions as or more general than "$\{x \mid 0 \leq x \leq 5\}$" and as or less general than "$\{x \mid -1000 < x < 1000\}$" and VS_2 contains all concept definitions as or more general than "$\{x \mid 5 \leq x \leq 10\}$" and as or less general than "$\{x \mid -1000 < x < 1000\}$," then the intersection of these is still a subset of the concept description language but is no longer bounded. The problem is that $\text{Min}(VS_1 \cap VS_2)$ is empty. The desired minimal element for the intersection would ideally have been "$\{x \mid 0 \leq x \leq 10\}$," but this is not in the language.

When the intersection of two version spaces is indeed bounded, and hence a version space, rather than explicitly intersecting the two version spaces by enumerating each of their elements, it is possible to compute the boundary sets for the intersection directly from the boundary sets of the two original version spaces. This is done by finding the minimal common generalizations of pairs of S-set elements for the new S-set and the maximal common specializations of pairs of G-set elements for the new G-set, and removing the overly general elements from the new S-set and overly specific elements from the new G-set (Section 2.3). To state this formally it is necessary to present what the most specific common generalizations (MSG) and most general common specializations (MGS) of two concept definitions are:

$$\text{MSG}(A,B) = \{C \mid A \preceq C \text{ and } B \preceq C \text{ and there is no } D$$
$$\text{such that } D \prec C \text{ with } A \preceq D \text{ and } B \preceq D\}$$
$$\text{MGS}(A,B) = \{C \mid C \preceq A \text{ and } C \preceq B \text{ and there is no } D$$
$$\text{such that } C \prec D \text{ with } D \preceq A \text{ and } D \preceq B\}.$$

It is now possible to state how the boundary sets for the intersection of two version spaces, when it is itself a version space, can be computed. The new boundary set $S_{1 \cap 2}$ contains the minimal common generalizations of pairs from S_1 and S_2 that are less than at least one element from each of G_1 and G_2, only maintaining the minimal ones from this set. $G_{1 \cap 2}$ is determined in a similar manner. More formally:

> **Theorem 8.6 (Version-Space Merging Algorithm):** *If $VS_1 \cap VS_2$ is bounded, then $\text{Min}(VS_1 \cap VS_2) = S_{1 \cap 2}$ and $\text{Max}(VS_1 \cap VS_2) = G_{1 \cap 2}$, where $S_{1 \cap 2}$ and $G_{1 \cap 2}$ are determined as follows:*

$$S_{1 \cap 2} = \text{Min}(\{s \in \text{MSG}(s_1, s_2) \mid s_1 \in S_1 \text{ and }$$
$$s_2 \in S_2, \text{ and } \exists g_1 \in G_1, g_2 \in G_2$$
$$\text{with } s \preceq g_1 \text{ and } s \preceq g_2\})$$

and

$$G_{1 \cap 2} = \text{Max}(\{g \in \text{MGS}(g_1, g_2) \mid g_1 \in G_1 \text{ and }$$
$$g_2 \in G_2, \text{ and } \exists s_1 \in S_1, s_2 \in S_2$$
$$\text{with } s_1 \preceq g \text{ and } s_2 \preceq g\}).$$

Proof: This is done for the S-set case (the proof for the G-set case is analogous) by first showing that $S_{1 \cap 2} \subseteq \mathrm{Min}(VS_1 \cap VS_2)$, then showing $S_{1 \cap 2} \supseteq \mathrm{Min}(VS_1 \cap VS_2)$. Both cases use the following lemma:

> **Lemma 8.1:** $c \in \{s \in \mathrm{MSG}(s_1, s_2) \mid s_1 \in S_1 \text{ and } s_2 \in S_2, \text{ and } \exists g_1 \in G_1, g_2 \in G_2 \text{ with } s \preceq g_1 \text{ and } s \preceq g_2\}$ *implies* $c \in VS_{1 \cap 2}$.

> **Proof:** $c \in \{s \in \mathrm{MSG}(s_1, s_2) \mid s_1 \in S_1 \text{ and } s_2 \in S_2, \text{ and } \exists g_1 \in G_1, g_2 \in G_2 \text{ with } s \preceq g_1 \text{ and } s \preceq g_2\}$ means $c \in \mathrm{MSG}(s_1, s_2)$ for some $s_1 \in S_1$ and $s_2 \in S_2$. This means $s_1 \preceq c$ and $s_2 \preceq c$ (by the definition of MSG), which shows that c has some element from each of the two original S-sets below it. But furthermore $c \in \{s \in \mathrm{MSG}(s_1, s_2) \mid s_1 \in S_1 \text{ and } s_2 \in S_2, \text{ and } \exists g_1 \in G_1, g_2 \in G_2 \text{ with } s \preceq g_1 \text{ and } s \preceq g_2\}$ means $\exists g_1 \in G_1, g_2 \in G_2 \text{ with } c \preceq g_1 \text{ and } c \preceq g_2$, which shows that c has some element from each of the two original G-sets below it. Therefore $c \in VS_1$ and $c \in VS_2$, and so $c \in VS_1 \cap VS_2$. □

First the $\subseteq$: If $c \in S_{1 \cap 2}$, then $c \in \{s \in \mathrm{MSG}(s_1, s_2) \mid s_1 \in S_1 \text{ and } s_2 \in S_2, \text{ and } \exists g_1 \in G_1, g_2 \in G_2 \text{ with } s \preceq g_1 \text{ and } s \preceq g_2\}$, so $c \in VS_1 \cap VS_2$ by Lemma 8.1. To show that $c \in \mathrm{Min}(VS_1 \cap VS_2)$ it is necessary to show that there is no $c' \prec c$ with $c' \in VS_1 \cap VS_2$. If there were some $c' \in VS_1 \cap VS_2$ with $c' \prec c$, there would be some $s \in \mathrm{Min}(VS_1 \cap VS_2)$ with $s \preceq c'$ (potentially $s = c'$), since $VS_1 \cap VS_2$ is bounded. This would mean that $s \prec c$, and it is therefore sufficient to show that $s \in \{s \in \mathrm{MSG}(s_1, s_2) \mid s_1 \in S_1 \text{ and } s_2 \in S_2, \text{ and } \exists g_1 \in G_1, g_2 \in G_2 \text{ with } s \preceq g_1 \text{ and } s \preceq g_2\}$, since this would contradict the fact that c is a minimal element of this set ($c \in S_{1 \cap 2}$).

$s \in \mathrm{Min}(VS_1 \cap VS_2)$ means $s \in VS_1 \cap VS_2$, so $s \in VS_1$ and $s \in VS_2$. This in turn means there is some $s_1 \in S_1$ and some $s_2 \in S_2$ with $s_1 \preceq s$ and $s_2 \preceq s$. Finally, there is no $s' \prec s$ with $s_1 \preceq s'$ and $s_2 \preceq s'$ (otherwise s' would be in $VS_1 \cap VS_2$, and so s would not be in $\mathrm{Min}(VS_1 \cap VS_2)$). Thus $s \in \mathrm{MSG}(s_1, s_2)$, and since s is in VS_1 and in VS_2 there is some $g_1 \in G_1$ and some $g_2 \in G_2$ with $s \preceq g_1$ and $s \preceq g_2$. Therefore $s \in \{s \in \mathrm{MSG}(s_1, s_2) \mid s_1 \in S_1 \text{ and } s_2 \in S_2, \text{ and } \exists g_1 \in G_1, g_2 \in G_2 \text{ with } s \preceq g_1$

and $s \preceq g_2$}, which contradicts the fact that c is a minimal element of this set.

For the $\supseteq$: If $c \in \mathrm{Min}(VS_1 \cap VS_2)$, then $c \in VS_1 \cap VS_2$. This means that $c \in VS_1$ and $c \in VS_2$, and furthermore there is some $s_1 \in S_1$ and some $s_2 \in S_2$ with $s_1 \preceq c$ and $s_2 \preceq c$. Finally, there is no $c' \prec c$ with $s_1 \preceq c'$ and $s_2 \preceq c'$ (otherwise c' would be in $VS_1 \cap VS_2$, and so c would not be in $\mathrm{Min}(VS_1 \cap VS_2)$). Thus $c \in \mathrm{MSG}(s_1, s_2)$, and since c is in VS_1 and in VS_2 there is some $g_1 \in G_1$ and some $g_2 \in G_2$ with $c \preceq g_1$ and $c \preceq g_2$. Therefore $c \in \{s \in \mathrm{MSG}(s_1, s_2) \mid s_1 \in S_1$ and $s_2 \in S_2$, and $\exists g_1 \in G_1$, $g_2 \in G_2$ with $s \preceq g_1$ and $s \preceq g_2\}$.

To show that that c is a minimal element of this set, and thus in $S_{1 \cap 2}$, it is necessary to show that there is no $c' \in \{s \in \mathrm{MSG}(s_1, s_2) \mid s_1 \in S_1$ and $s_2 \in S_2$, and $\exists g_1 \in G_1, g_2 \in G_2$ with $s \preceq g_1$ and $s \preceq g_2\}$ with $c' \prec c$. This is true because if there were such a c', it would be in $VS_1 \cap VS_2$ (by Lemma 8.1), which would mean that c is not in $\mathrm{Min}(VS_1 \cap VS_2)$, which would be a contradiction. $\square$

Note that Theorem 8.6 presents a method for computing intersections in theory, but to be practical the computations must take a finite amount of time. In particular, computing $\mathrm{MSG}(s_1, s_2)$ must take a finite amount of time. If there are infinite chains in the concept description language, the procedure for computing MSG might never halt if it traverses the partial order. Thus in real applications MSG will often be computed from the syntactic form of s_1 and s_2, rather than traversing the partial order. For example, to determine $\mathrm{MSG}(\{x \mid a_1 \le x \le b_1\}, \{x \mid a_2 \le x \le b_2\})$ a procedure for computing MSG directly from the partial order would never halt, since there are an infinite number of concept definitions more general than each of the concept definitions. However, it is a simple matter to compute their most specific common generalization from their syntactic form: $\{x \mid min(a_1, a_2) \le x \le max(b_1, b_2)\}$. Typically MSG is defined for specific concept description languages to manipulate the syntactic structures so it need not face infinite-chain difficulties.

8.4   Version-Space Unions

This section discusses unions of version spaces, and presents conditions under which the union of two version spaces is a version space, as well as a method for doing unions in boundary-set representation. It is first useful to note that the union of two version spaces is always bounded:

> **Theorem 8.7:**   *Given two version spaces VS_1 and VS_2, their union $VS_1 \cup VS_2$ is bounded.*

Proof: For any $c \in VS_1 \cup VS_2$, either $c \in VS_1$ or $c \in VS_2$. Without loss of generality, assume $c \in VS_1$. To show that $VS_1 \cup VS_2$ is bounded, it is necessary to show that there is some $s \in \text{Min}(VS_1 \cup VS_2)$ with $s \preceq c$. The proof that there is some $g \in \text{Max}(VS_1 \cup VS_2)$ with $c \preceq g$ is analogous.

Since $c \in VS_1$, there is some $s \in S_1$ with $s \preceq c$. Either $s \in \text{Min}(VS_1 \cup VS_2)$, in which case there is some $s \in \text{Min}(VS_1 \cup VS_2)$ with $s \preceq c$, or else $s \notin \text{Min}(VS_1 \cup VS_2)$. If this latter case is true, there must be some $c' \in VS_1 \cup VS_2$ with $c' \prec s$. Since s is in S_1, c' must be in VS_2. But VS_2 is a version space, and hence bounded, so there is some $s' \in S_2$ with $s' \preceq c'$. Since $c' \prec s$, this means $s' \prec s$. But $s \in S_1$, so there is no $c'' \in VS_1$ with $c'' \prec s'$. Also, there is no $c'' \in VS_2$ with $c'' \prec s'$ (since $s' \in S_2$). This means $s' \in \text{Min}(VS_1 \cup VS_2)$. Thus for any $c \in VS_1 \cup VS_2$ there is some $s \in \text{Min}(VS_1 \cup VS_2)$ with $s \preceq c$. $\square$

A simple corollary of this is

> **Corollary 8.2:**   *The union of two version spaces is a version space if and only if the union is closed.*

Note that just as the intersection of two version spaces need not be a version space, similarly the union of two version spaces need not be a version space. To see this consider any concept description language with three elements $c_1 \prec c_2 \prec c_3$. Let $VS_1 = \{c_1\}$ and $VS_2 = \{c_3\}$. The union of the two version spaces is $\{c_1, c_3\}$, but this doesn't include c_2, which it must if it is to be closed and a version space.

Just as for intersections, the minimal and maximal elements for the union of two version spaces can be determined directly from the boundary sets for the two version spaces being unioned. These form the boundary sets for the union when the union is closed and thus a version space.

Theorem 8.8 (Version-Space Union Algorithm):

$$\text{Min}(VS_1 \cup VS_2) = S_{1\cup2} \text{ and } \text{Max}(VS_1 \cup VS_2) = G_{1\cup2},$$

where

$$S_{1\cup2} = \text{Min}(S_1 \cup S_2)$$

and

$$G_{1\cup2} = \text{Max}(G_1 \cup G_2).$$

Proof: This is done for $S_{1\cup2}$ by first showing that $S_{1\cup2} \subseteq \text{Min}(VS_1 \cup VS_2)$, then showing that $S_{1\cup2} \supseteq \text{Min}(VS_1 \cup VS_2)$. The proof for $G_{1\cup2}$ is analogous.

For the $\subseteq$: If $c \in S_{1\cup2}$, then $c \in \text{Min}(S_1 \cup S_2)$. This means c is in $S_1 \cup S_2$, which in turn means $c \in S_1$ or $c \in S_2$, and thus $c \in VS_1$ or $c \in VS_2$. Hence $c \in VS_1 \cup VS_2$. To show that c is a minimal element of this set it is necessary to show that there is no $c' \in VS_1 \cup VS_2$ with $c' \prec c$. Assume there is such a c'. Then it is either in VS_1 or VS_2. Without loss of generality assume it is in VS_1. Then there must be some $s_1 \in S_1$ with $s \preceq c'$ (since VS_1 is a version space). This s_1 is in S_1, so it is in $S_1 \cup S_2$. But since $s_1 \preceq c' \prec c$, c cannot be in $\text{Min}(S_1 \cup S_2)$. This is a contradiction. Therefore there is no $c' \in VS_1 \cup VS_2$ with $c' \prec c$, and thus $c \in \text{Min}(VS_1 \cup VS_2)$

For the $\supseteq$: If $c \in \text{Min}(VS_1 \cup VS_2)$, then $c \in VS_1 \cup VS_2$ and there is no $c' \in VS_1 \cup VS_2$ with $c' \prec c$. This means $c \in VS_1$ or $c \in VS_2$. Assume $c \in VS_1$. c must in S_1, since c is in $\text{Min}(VS_1 \cup VS_2)$, which means there is no $c' \in VS_1$ with $c' \prec c$. The case for $c \in VS_2$ is analogous. Thus $c \in S_1 \cup S_2$. Furthermore, there is no $c'' \in S_1 \cup S_2$ with $c'' \prec c$ (otherwise c would not be in $\text{Min}(VS_1 \cup VS_2)$, since $c'' \in S_1 \cup S_2$ means $c'' \in VS_1 \cup VS_2$). Thus $c \in S_{1\cup2}$. $\square$

Note that although this presents a method for computing unions of version spaces, for many purposes the union can be computed directly without generating individual version spaces and then using the algorithm to merge them. Dealing with ambiguous data (Chapter 3) is one example where this occurs. It creates a union of multiple version spaces without explicitly generating individual version spaces and using the union algorithm on them.

8.5 Summary

This chapter has presented formal results on the range of applicability of the generalization of version spaces developed in this work. It analyzed when such version spaces can be intersected and unioned, gave methods to do so in boundary-set representation, and proved that the algorithms to do so are correct.

Chapter 9

Conclusions

The problem of concept learning—forming general rules from specific cases—has received much attention in artificial intelligence. This book has presented a general framework for concept learning based on a generalization of Mitchell's version-space approach that removes its assumption of strict consistency with data. This chapter concludes the book with a review of the principal results, an analysis of why incremental version-space merging works, and a discussion of open problems.

9.1 Results

The first contribution of this work is the generalized version-space framework, which has been shown to have firm theoretical underpinnings. Central to the framework is incremental version-space merging, an incremental learning method based on version-space intersection. For each piece of information, it forms the version space containing all concept definitions that are potentially relevant given the information, and intersects the version space with the version space based on all past data to obtain a new version space that reflects all the past data plus the new information. The generality of the learning method was demonstrated by its use on four very different learning tasks, all implemented using the single learning method. Two of these applications of incremental version-space merging stand as the additional contributions of this work.

97

The first application is the use of incremental version-space merging to solve a subset of the open problem of learning from inconsistent data in a computationally feasible manner using version spaces. The approach presented here succeeds in this task by identifying and addressing the subclass of the problem called "bounded inconsistency," which occurs when every nonrepresentative example has a neighboring example that is representative. The general approach is to form version spaces containing all concept definitions consistent with an instance or one of its neighbors. Incremental version-space merging intersects the version spaces generated in this manner for all the given data, which determines all concept definitions consistent with all examples or their neighbors.

The second application is the use of incremental version-space merging to combine empirical and analytical learning, solving problems they each have when used in isolation. The central idea is to apply explanation-based generalization (EBG) to training data and form version spaces consistent with the generalized data. Incremental version-space merging is then used on the resulting version spaces. From the perspective of analytical learning, the process permits learning even in the presence of imperfect domain theories. From the perspective of empirical learning the combination allows the use of knowledge as an explicit bias in learning. The result is a learning technique that performs along a spectrum from knowledge-free to knowledge-rich domains. The combination operates like empirical learning given no knowledge, but can utilize knowledge when provided. Given an incomplete theory (i.e., it only explains a subset of potential instances), when an explanation exists empirical learning works on the analytically generalized data; when no explanation can be found the learner utilizes the ground data. When there is no domain theory at all the hybrid approach degenerates to look like the candidate-elimination algorithm.

9.2   Analysis

The first question that must be asked of any system is whether it works. Here this question was answered with both experimentation and theory. Chapters 3 through 6 demonstrate the solution of four different learning tasks within the generalized version-space framework, including the significantly differing tasks of learning from inconsistent data and combining empirical and analytical learning. In all four cases the learning task was solved using incremental version-space merging. Chapter 8 complements this empirical validation with a formal analysis of the technique, proving that the version-space merging algorithm does actually compute what it is supposed to, the intersection of two version spaces. Thus the success of the technique was demonstrated both empirically and analytically.

Chapter 8 furthermore discussed the theoretical limits on when the approach described in this book will apply at all. Two terms were defined. A subset of a concept description language is closed if, given two concept definitions in the set, all other concept definitions between them are also in the set. A subset of a concept description language is bounded if all concept definitions in the set have some concept definition among the set's minimal items below it and some concept definition among the set's maximal items above it. If a subset of the concept description language is both closed and bounded the set is representable by boundary sets, and the incremental version-space merging learning method can apply. If the desired set of concept definitions for a single piece of information is not bounded or closed, incremental version-space merging will not apply. One area for future work is to extend incremental version-space merging to handle arbitrary sets of concept definitions.

However, in addition to whether the approach even applies, there is the additional question of whether the approach is computationally feasible. Chapter 7 discussed this issue, and included an analysis of the computational complexity of the approach. Although in the worst case incremental version-space merging has complexity exponential in the number of instances, the chapter gives heuristic techniques for dealing with computational intractability. Arguments are also given there for why the worst-case complexity need not always occur.

9.3   Open Problems

There are a number of interesting directions in which this work can be extended. The first, mentioned in the previous section, is to extend incremental version-space merging to handle arbitrary sets of concepts. One approach would be to represent arbitrary sets as nested differences of version spaces. The intersection procedure could utilize facts such as $(A - B) \cap (C - D) = (A \cap C) - (B \cup D)$, as well as simplifications such as $A - B = A$ if $A \cap B = \emptyset$, and $(A - \emptyset) = A$. Ultimately operations will bottom out at intersections and unions of version spaces.

Chapter 4 presented a method for learning from inconsistent data, and Chapter 5 described how empirical and analytical learning can be combined using incremental version-space merging. An interesting open problem is to combine the two approaches. In general this is a very hard problem. If the result of learning is incorrect, the question to answer is whether it is due to anomalous data or incorrect domain knowledge. Handling subcases of the general problem seems feasible, such as when there is some knowledge about whether the data or the knowledge is more believable. For example, if the domain theory for positive data is known to cover all positive examples (and perhaps additional data, such as is the case with explanatory theories), then when a positive instance cannot be explained the instance is instead known to be negative.

Finally, the most important problem faced by incremental version-space merging, and concept learning more generally, is when the concept description language is inadequate. If the desired concept cannot be expressed, the desired concept cannot be learned. There are two situations where this occurs. The first is when the correct primitives are provided, but the limited ways for combining the primitives do not include the desired concept. One possible solution to this is to instead form an approximation of the desired concept in the given language (e.g., Haussler, 1988; Amsterdam, 1988). A second approach is to use failure in the given language to suggest extensions to the language that would allow successful learning (e.g., Utgoff, 1986). There is much work to be done in this important area.

The second case where the desired concept cannot be expressed is when a necessary primitive is not provided. This seems almost definitionally impossible—how can a blind man learn about red blocks? One approach to handling this would be to discover new means by which the feature can actually be observed. For example, a blind man can ask a sighted person to identify the color of a block. However, in some cases there will just be no way to identify the missing feature.

9.4 Summary

This work has shown how a generalization of Mitchell's version-space approach to concept learning that removes its assumption of strict consistency with data can be successfully applied to a wide range of learning tasks beyond those to which the original version-space approach can be applied. For a particular learning task the user must define what sets of concept definitions are relevant given each piece of information. Incremental version-space merging takes these version spaces and intersects them as they are obtained using the version-space merging algorithm to yield the set of all concept definitions that reflect all the obtained data.

The first application of this generalized approach was to demonstrate that it still maintains the functionality of the original approach, and to extend the method to apply to a more general class of data, when data are ambiguous. A second application, which serves as a contribution of this work in its own right, uses the generalized approach to learn from data with bounded inconsistency—a subclass of inconsistent data identified and exploited in this work. Finally, a very different application of incremental version-space merging, which also serves as a contribution of this work, is to use explanation-based generalization in learning, developing a method that works along a spectrum from knowledge-poor to knowledge-rich domains.

In summary, this book has presented a new, generalized framework for concept learning. The observation on which all the results are based is that concept learning can be viewed as the two-step process of specifying sets of relevant concepts and intersecting these sets. This observation is ultimately the major contribution of this work.

Appendix A

IVSM Program Listing

This appendix contains a Prolog implementation of incremental version-space merging. First is the code for the general loop for incremental version-space merging, `process_data_1(InstanceList,OldS, OldG,NewS,NewG)`; it corresponds directly to the three-step loop in Section 2.3. It forms the instance version space for the next instance in `InstanceList` then uses the version-space merging code (`vs_new`) to merge it with the version space for past data (boundary sets `OldS` and `OldG`), returning the new boundary sets in `NewS` and `NewG`. `inst_vs` should be defined as appropriate for each learning task; for example, `inst_vs` called explanation-based generalization to form the instance version space for the learning tasks in Chapter 5.

```
process_data_1([I|R],S1,G1,S,G):-
    inst_vs(I,S2,G2),
    vs_new(S1,G1,S2,G2,S3,G3),
    process_data_1(R,S3,G3,S,G).
process_data_1([],S,G,S,G).
```

The version-space merging code `vs_new` first checks that the version space for past data is not a subset of the new version space (Section 7.3.2). If it is, it simply returns the old version space, since that's what version-space merging would generate anyway. This saves time, since the subset test is relatively inexpensive compared to the more costly merging process.

```
vs_new(SA,GA,SB,GB,SA,GA) :-
```

```
    subset(SA,GA,SB,GB),!.
```

subset (SA, GA, SB, GB) tests whether one version space (with boundary set SA and GA) is a subset of a second version space (with boundary set
SB and GB). It checks if each member of GA has some element of GB above
it and if each member of SA has some element of SB below it. le_test
checks whether one concept definition is equal to or more specific than
a second, and is defined as appropriate for the given concept description
language. It can assume that its arguments will both be bound to actual
concept definitions.

```
    subset(SA,GA,SB,GB):-
        checktop(GA,GB),
        checkbottom(SA,SB).
    checktop([],GB).
    checktop([H|T],GB):-
        member(X,GB),
        le_test(H,X),
        checktop(T,GB).
    checkbottom([],SB).
    checkbottom([H|T],SB):-
        member(X,SB),
        le_test(X,H),
        checkbottom(T,SB).
```

vs_new (SA, GA, SB, GB, S, G) implements the version-space merging algorithm (Section 2.2). It intersects the version space with boundary
sets SA and GA with the version space with boundary sets SB and GB, returning the result as S and G. It first generates the new *S*-set, then the new
G-set:

```
    vs_new(SA,GA,SB,GB,S,G):-
        s_new(SA,GA,SB,GB,S),
        g_new(SA,GA,SB,GB,G).
```

s_new (SA, GA, SB, GB, S) determines the most specific common generalizations of pairs from SA and SB that are covered by some element
of GA and some element of GB (using covered_msg), and returns the

minimal elements of this set (since the `covered_msg` of one pair may be more general than that generated by another pair) as the new *S*-set S. `g_new` is comparable.

```
s_new(SA,GA,SB,GB,S):-
    bagof(X,covered_msg(SA,SB,GA,GB,X),A),
    minimal_elements(A,S).
covered_msg(SA,SB,GA,GB,X):-
    member(A,SA),member(B,SB),msg(A,B,C),
    member(X,C),
    member(D,GA),le_test(X,D),
    member(E,GB),le_test(X,E).
g_new(SA,GA,SB,GB,G):-
    bagof(X,covering_mgs(SA,SB,GA,GB,X),A),
    maximal_elements(A,G).
covering_mgs(SA,SB,GA,GB,X):-
    member(A,GA),member(B,GB),mgs(A,B,C),
    member(X,C),
    member(D,SA),le_test(D,X),
    member(E,SB),le_test(E,X).
```

Like `le_test`, `msg` and `mgs` are defined as appropriate for the given concept description language. `msg` determines the set of most specific common generalizations of two concept definitions, and similarly `mgs` should determine the most general common specialization of two concept definitions.

Finally `minimal_elements(A,G)` collects in G the minimal elements of A in the order defined by `lt_test`, where `lt_test` checks whether one concept definition is more specific than a second (it is similar to `le_test`, but without the test of equality). It first finds the most specific elements of G, then removes duplicates. The definition for `maximal_elements(A,G)` is comparable.

```
minimal_elements(A,G):-
    most_spec_elements(A,B),
    uniq_elements(B,G).
most_spec_elements(A,B):-
```

```
    bagof(X,min_element(X,A),B).
min_element(X,S):-
    member(X,S),
    not smaller_element_in(X,S).
smaller_element_in(X,S):-
    member(Y,S),
    lt_test(Y,X).
maximal_elements(A,G):-
    most_gen_elements(A,B),
    uniq_elements(B,G).
most_gen_elements(A,B):-
    bagof(X,max_element(X,A),B).
max_element(X,S):-
    member(X,S),
    not bigger_element_in(X,S).
bigger_element_in(X,S):-
    member(Y,S),
    lt_test(X,Y).
uniq_elements([A|B],C):-
    member(A,B),!,
    uniq_elements(B,C).
uniq_elements([A|B],[A|C]):-
    uniq_elements(B,C).
uniq_elements([A],[A]).
```

Bibliography

1. D. W. Aha and D. Kibler. Detecting and removing noisy instances from concept descriptions. Technical Report 88-12, University of California, Irvine, 1989.

2. J. B. Amsterdam. Extending the Valiant learning model. In *Proceedings of the Fifth International Machine Learning Conference*, pages 381–394, Ann Arbor, Michigan, June 1988.

3. J. R. Anderson. *The Architecture of Cognition*. Harvard University Press, Cambridge, MA, 1983.

4. J. R. Anderson. Knowledge compilation: The general learning mechanism. In R. S. Michalski, J. G. Carbonell, and T. M. Mitchell, editors, *Machine Learning: An Artificial Intelligence Approach, Volume II*, pages 289–310. Morgan Kaufmann, Los Altos, CA, 1986.

5. B. G. Buchanan and T. M. Mitchell. Model-directed learning of production rules. In D. A. Waterman and F. Hayes-Roth, editors, *Pattern-Directed Inference Systems*, pages 297–312. Academic Press, New York, 1978.

6. B. G. Buchanan, J. Sullivan, T.-P. Cheng, and S. H. Clearwater. Simulation-assisted inductive learning. In *Proceedings of the National Conference on Artificial Intelligence*, pages 552–557, Minneapolis, Minnesota, August 1988.

7. S. H. Clearwater, T.-P. Cheng, H. Hirsh, and B. G. Buchanan. Incremental batch learning. In *Proceedings of the Sixth International*

Workshop on Machine Learning, pages 366–370, Ithaca, New York, 1989.

8.   W. W. Cohen. *Explanation-Based Generalization as an Abstraction Mechanism in Concept Learning*. PhD thesis, Rutgers University, 1990 (expected).

9.   A. P. Danyluk. The use of explanations for similarity-based learning. In *Proceedings of the Tenth International Joint Conference on Artificial Intelligence*, Milan, Italy, August 1987.

10. B. V. Dasarathy. Nosing around the neighborhood: A new system structure and classification rule for recognition in partially exposed environments. *PAMI*, PAMI-2(1):67–71, January 1980.

11. R. Davis. Applications of meta-level knowledge to the construction, maintenance and use of large knowledge bases. In R. Davis and D. Lenat, editors, *Knowledge-Based Systems in Artificial Intelligence*. McGraw-Hill, New York, New York, 1982.

12. G. F. DeJong and R. Mooney. Explanation-based learning: An alternative view. *Machine Learning*, 1(2):145–176, 1986.

13. T. G. Dietterich, B. London, K. Clarkson, and G. Dromey. Learning and inductive inference. In P. Cohen and E. A. Feigenbaum, editors, *The Handbook of Artificial Intelligence, Volume III*. William Kaufmann, Los Altos, CA, 1982.

14. G. Drastal, R. Meunier, and S. Raatz. Error correction in constructive induction. In *Proceedings of the Sixth International Workshop on Machine Learning*, pages 81–83, Ithaca, New York, 1989.

15. R. A. Fisher. The use of multiple measurements in taxonomic problems. *Annual Eugenics*, 7:179–188, 1936. Also in *Contributions to Mathematical Statistics*, John Wiley & Sons, NY, 1950.

16. N. S. Flann and T. G. Dietterich. A study of explanation-based methods for inductive learning. *Machine Learning*, 4(1), 1990.

17. L.-M. Fu. *Learning Object-Level and Meta-Level Knowledge for Expert Systems*. PhD thesis, Stanford University, 1985.

18. D. Haussler. Quantifying the inductive bias in concept learning. In *Proceedings of the National Conference on Artificial Intelligence*, pages 485–489, Philadelphia, PA, August 1986.

19. D. Haussler. Quantifying inductive bias: AI learning algorithms and Valiant's learning framework. *Artificial Intelligence*, 26(2):177–221, Sept. 1988.

20. H. Hirsh. Reasoning about operationality for explanation-based learning. In *Proceedings of the Fifth International Machine Learning Conference*, pages 214–220, Ann Arbor, Michigan, June 1988.

21. J. E. Laird, P. S. Rosenbloom, and A. Newell. Chunking in Soar: The anatomy of a general learning mechanism. *Machine Learning*, 1(1):11–46, 1986.

22. M. Lebowitz. Integrated learning: Controlling explanation. *Cognitive Science*, 10(2), 1986.

23. S. Marcus, editor. *Automating Knowledge Acquisition for Expert Systems*. Kluwer, Boston, MA, 1988.

24. R. S. Michalski and R. L. Chilausky. Learning by being told and learning from examples: An experimental comparison of the two methods of knowledge acquisition in the context of developing an expert system for soybean disease diagnosis. *Policy Analysis and Information Systems*, 4(3):219–244, September 1980.

25. R. S. Michalski and J. B. Larson. Selection of most representative training examples and incremental generation of vl1 hypotheses: The underlying methodology and description of programs esel and aq11. Report 867, University of Illinois, 1978.

26. R. S. Michalski. A theory and methodology of inductive learning. In R. S. Michalski, J. G. Carbonell, and T. M. Mitchell, editors, *Machine Learning: An Artificial Intelligence Approach*, pages 83–134. Morgan Kaufmann, Los Altos, CA, 1983.

27. T. M. Mitchell, P. E. Utgoff, and R. B. Banerji. Learning by experimentation: Acquiring and refining problem-solving heuristics. In R. S. Michalski, J. G. Carbonell, and T. M. Mitchell, editors, *Machine Learning: An Artificial Intelligence Approach*, pages 163–190. Morgan Kaufmann, Los Altos, CA, 1983.

28. T. M. Mitchell, S. Mahadevan, and L. I. Steinberg. LEAP: A learning apprentice for VLSI design. In *Proceedings of the Ninth International Joint Conference on Artificial Intelligence*, Los Angeles, CA, August 1985.

29. T. M. Mitchell, L. I. Steinberg, and J. S. Shulman. A knowledge-based approach to design. *IEEE Transactions on Pattern Analysis and Machine Intelligence*, PAMI-7(5):502–510, September 1985.

30. T. M. Mitchell, R. M. Keller, and S. T. Kedar-Cabelli. Explanation-based generalization: A unifying view. *Machine Learning*, 1(1):47–80, 1986.

31. T. M. Mitchell. Version spaces: A candidate elimination approach to rule learning. In *Proceedings of the Fifth International Joint Conference on Artificial Intelligence*, volume 1, pages 305–310, MIT, Cambridge, MA, August 1977.

32. T. M. Mitchell. *Version Spaces: An Approach to Concept Learning*. PhD thesis, Stanford University, December 1978.

33. T. M. Mitchell. The need for biases in learning generalizations. Technical Report CBM-TR-117, Department of Computer Science, Rutgers University, May 1980.

34. T. M. Mitchell. Generalization as search. *Artificial Intelligence*, 18(2):203–226, March 1982.

35. T. M. Mitchell. Toward combining empirical and analytic methods for learning heuristics. In A. Elithorn and R. Banerji, editors, *Human and Artificial Intelligence*. Erlbaum, 1984. Also Rutgers Laboratory for CS Research Memo LCSR-TR-27, Mar 1982.

36. M. Pazzani. *Learning Causal Relationships: An Integration of Empirical and Explanation-Based Learning Methods*. PhD thesis, University of California, Los Angeles, 1988.

37. J. R. Quinlan. Learning efficient classification procedures and their application to chess end-games. In R. S. Michalski, J. G. Carbonell, and T. M. Mitchell, editors, *Machine Learning: An Artificial Intelligence Approach*, pages 463–482. Morgan Kaufmann, Los Altos, CA, 1983.

38. J. R. Quinlan. The effect of noise on concept learning. In R. S. Michalski, J. G. Carbonell, and T. M. Mitchell, editors, *Machine Learning: An Artificial Intelligence Approach, Volume II*, pages 149–166. Morgan Kaufmann, Los Altos, CA, 1986.

39. J. R. Quinlan. Decision trees as probabilistic classfiers. In *Proceedings of the Fourth International Machine Learning Workshop*, pages 31–37, Irvine, CA, June 1987.

40. P. S. Rosenbloom and J. E. Laird. Mapping explanation-based generalization onto Soar. In *Proceedings of the National Conference on Artificial Intelligence*, pages 561–567, Philadelphia, PA, August 1986.

41. P. S. Rosenbloom, J. E. Laird, and A. Newell. Knowledge-level learning in Soar. In *Proceedings of the National Conference on Artificial Intelligence*, Seattle, Washington, July 1987.

42. S. J. Russell and B. N. Grosof. A declarative approach to bias in concept learning. In *Proceedings of the National Conference on Artificial Intelligence*, Seattle, Washington, July 1987.

43. S. J. Russell. Analogy and single-instance generalization. In *Proceedings of the Fourth International Machine Learning Workshop*, pages 383–389, Irvine, CA, June 1987.

44. H. Simon and G. Lea. Problem solving and rule induction. In H. Simon, editor, *Models of Thought*. Yale University Press, 1974.

45. P. E. Utgoff. *Machine Learning of Inductive Bias*. Kluwer, Boston, MA, 1986.

46. F. van Harmelen and A. Bundy. Explanation-based generalisation
    = partial evaluation. *Artificial Intelligence*, 36(3):401–412, October
    1988.

47. P. H. Winston. Learning structural descriptions from examples. In
    P. H. Winston, editor, *The Psychology of Computer Vision*, page
    Chapter 5. McGraw Hill, New York, 1975.

Index